MW00624425

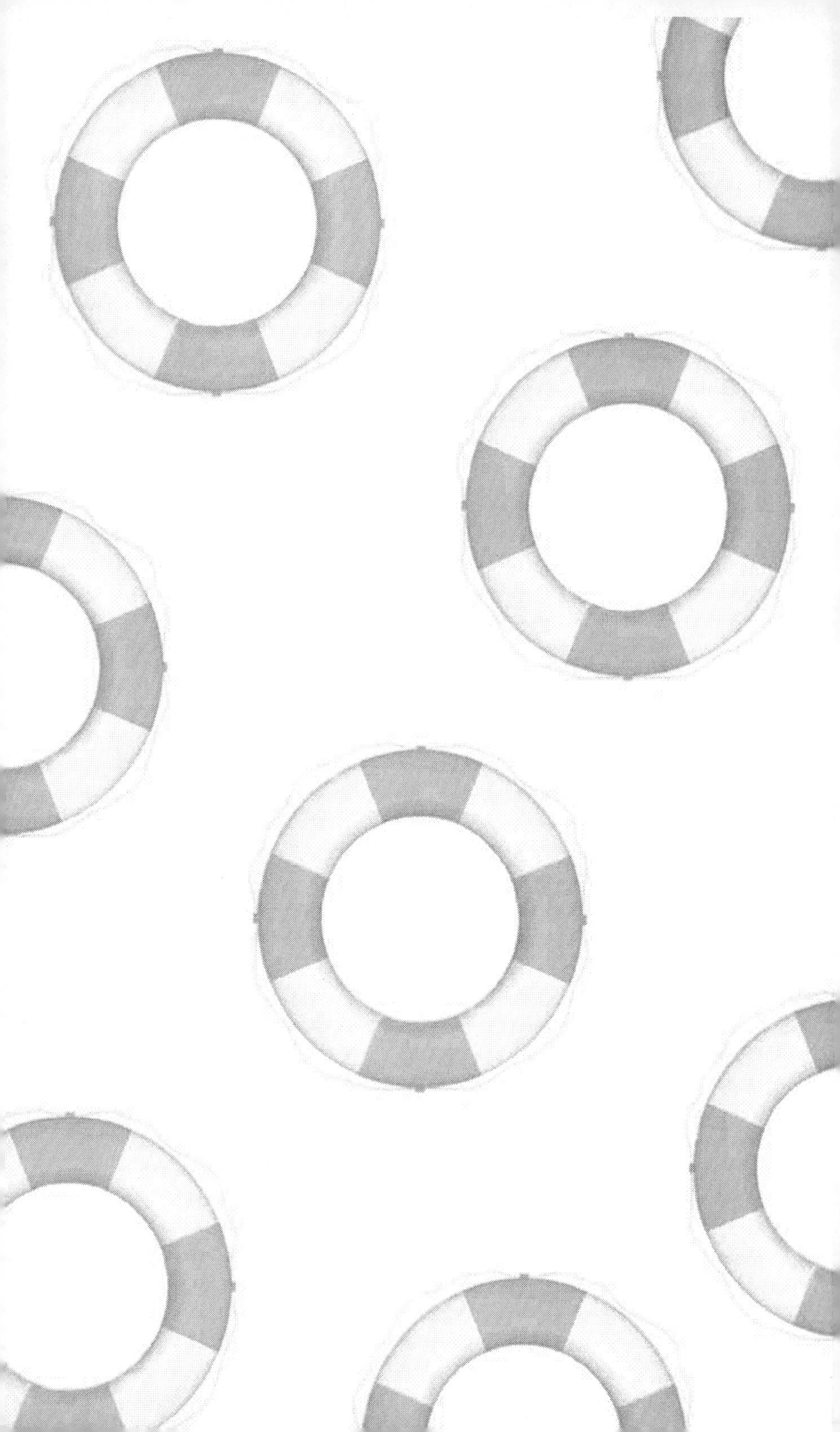

Everything I Wanted to Know About Credit

Wealth Builders Enterprises, Inc
525 N. Tryon St. Suite 1619
Charlotte, NC 28202
www.wealthbuildersnc.com
Phone: 877-279-9922
Fax: 704-973-0062
Email: brian@wealthbuildersnc.com

Published by A Better World Publishing, Inc.
www.everythingaboutcredit.com
HELP! I'm Drowning in Debt
Written by: Brian P. Willis and Angela B. Willis

Printed in the United States of America

Library of Congress Cataloguing-in-Publication Data

Willis Brian and Willis, Angela
Help I'm drowning in debt: everything I wanted to know about credit / Brian Willis and Angela Willis / 1st pbk ed.

p. cm.
ISBN 0-615-30196-9: $24.95
1. Finance – Credit. 2. Finance – Debt. 3. Finance – Budgeting. 4. Success – Psychological Aspects. 4. Problem Solving. 5. Self Improvement. I. Title.

First Edition: July 2009

10 9 8 7 6 5 4 3 2

Printed in the United States of America

I want to dedicate this book to my wife. This book would not have happened had it not been for her. My son James and I are both successful (as a family) because of this woman. God has given me many things in my life but the blessing that I appreciate most is my Angela.

CONTENTS

Online glossary available at
www.everythingaboutcredit.com

To: ____________________

From: ____________________

Date: ____________________

Personal Message:

____

____

____

____

____

____

____

____

Shortcut Key

This book is designed to help you through your journey of credit enlightenment and financial empowerment! I recommend that you read this book from cover to cover, in order to reap the full benefit of the information it contains. I am aware; however, that (statistically) people seldom read financial books from cover to cover, as they purchase them for specific reasons. Readers generally go directly to the area of importance for their situation. For the record, your reading every word in this book or only reading specific sections isn't my biggest concern. I simply want you to get the most out of what you read and make the information work for you!

For those who don't have the time, patience or energy to read the entire book, don't worry about it...I'm looking out for you too. Following is a short cut key that will navigate you through your topic of importance. Again, I recommend that you read the entire book for the full effect; most importantly however, I want you to succeed in your credit and financial management goals. Whatever route you take, make sure that you get the most out of this book and apply it to your life... for the rest of your life!

Shortcut Key

#	Area of Interest	Detail	Sessions to Read
1	Credit Education	I'd like to learn about the overall credit process. (History)	1, 3, 5, 6, 7, 8, 9, 11, 12
2	Credit Improvement	I have good credit but I want to improve my credit.	1, 9, 11, 12, 14, 15
3	Credit Maintenance	I'd like information about ongoing credit maintenance.	1, 7, 9, 11, 12, 14, 16
4	Financial Planning	I want information about budgeting and credit planning.	1, 3, 7, 9, 11, 12, 13 (College), 15
5	Commercial Credit	I want information about commercial credit.	1, 3, 5, 7, 8, 10, 15
6	High School Students	Credit and budgeting for High School Students	1, 2, 3, 7, 8, 9, 11, 12,13 (HS), 14,15
7	College Students	Credit and budgeting for College Students	1, 3, 4, 7, 8, 9, 11, 12,13 (College), 14,15
8	Identity Theft	I want more information about identity theft.	1, 7, 9, 11, 12, 15, 16
9	No Credit	I have no credit...how do I build credit? (Adults)	1, 3, 4, 7, 8, 9, 11, 12,13 (College), 14,15
10	Credit Repair	HELP! I have bad credit!	1, 7, 8, 9, 11, 12, 14, 15

Introduction

Although this book is not about the economic condition in the U.S. or theories around it; I would be remiss to not address the fact that our economic world has changed! Unless you've been hiding under a rock for the last three years, you are well aware of that fact by now. A massive credit crisis descended on America in 2007 and brought with it one of the most comprehensive financial, mental and social shifts that many of us will experience in our lifetimes. I can't predict what the economic and credit process will look like when the dust settles; however, I can confidently predict that the shift WILL shape the future of the credit process.

I am a student of history, economic trending, consumerism and common sense. It is my job to analyze economic shifts and trends that happened in the past, as well as predict and prepare for future shifts and trends. More importantly, as a critical thinker, it is my job to look beyond what I read study and hear and look at the human condition. One should never solely rely on facts and figures because there is always the human component to consider. As we all know human beings can throw a monkey wrench in the best laid plans of any economist; and the credit crisis is proof of that. I wish I could tell you that my research fully protected me from the effects of the burst of the housing bubble. I will also admit that it does not guarantee that I will be protected from future downward trends. I am just as vulnerable to the highs and lows of economic shifts as you. The difference is, although I've learned to expect the economic shifts, I don't waste time worrying about them when making business decisions. I have always relied on research, marketing, prayer and faith as a model for making business decisions and I don't plan to change that model, no matter what economic state this country is in.

I opened my property management firm in late 2006 because, from historical data and trending, it was evident that the housing boom would begin to subside by mid 2007. My forecasting and needs assessment revealed that people would soon require management for the many investment properties they had acquired when the banks were literally giving money away. Little did I know that within six short months the housing bubble would burst and send shockwaves across the world that would change the financial paradigm. By late 2007, my property management firm was suddenly a better investment than I'd anticipated. Unfortunately, it was due to so many people needing rental housing after massive foreclosures, instead of simple management of their investment properties. It wasn't the best time to open a new business, but I did the research, educated myself, prayed and moved forward. That is what you are doing by reading this book...you are moving forward!

Despite what's happening with our economy today, you clearly want to shift your economic future by improving your credit and financial outlook. I applaud you for that. This book is dedicated to the education of the credit process. We will also review trends in the financial market that will affect the credit process, giving us a possible look into the future of credit processing. My sole reason for writing this book is to offer information that will help you compete in an ever changing economy. The rules of finance are not the same for everybody, that is the simple truth, but the information is out there that can even the playing field. It's up to you to get that information. By purchasing this book and making a commitment to change your financial future you are on your way.

Remember that this is a journey! Think of this journey as a hands-on educational session but instead of paying hundreds of dollars, you get the information for the low low price of... this book☺ The information included is wide ranging and applies to everyone; however, the plan is personalized through the homework sessions. The personalized information that you create will put you on the path to full financial awareness. THIS WILL NOT BE AN OVERNIGHT PROCESS. Depending on your situation it may take a substantial amount of time, but think about this, if you do nothing, what will happen? Exactly... NOTHING!

I expect two things from you...

1) The determination to improve your situation!
I expect steely determination from you, which includes: a sincere desire to educate yourself, dedication to actively repairing credit issues, consistency in your actions and finally, a new mindset about maintaining your good credit.

2) Complete your homework!
You will be responsible for completing homework after each session. The homework is designed to enhance the information learned in each session and build your personal plan. By the end of this process, you will have compiled a personal financial and credit improvement plan, customized for your particular situation. The homework can be compiled in the accompanying Workbook or online in the E-book (the online workbook). Feel free to use a "dedicated" note-book if additional space is required.

VIRTUAL ASSISTANCE

I would love to conduct these sessions one-on-one; however, we know that it is impossible, given both of our busy schedules. I am therefore dispatching Virtual Brian to assist you. Virtual Brian is equipped with the same credentials that I have; over 20 years in the financial industry, Series 7, Series 64 and numerous other certifications, professional speaker, author, successful entrepreneur and credit specialist. As I guide you through your educational sessions, Virtual Brian will be your homework assistant. Let me forewarn you though... Virtual Brian is quite direct and to the point. Where I take a more delicate, tactful approach, Virtual Brian cuts to the chase and dispenses his version of the information as "Quick Hits". Virtual Brian is also available online to help with homework and general questions throughout your journey of credit education and improvement.

Remember... **YOU** are responsible for completing **YOUR** homework! It will help **YOU** get a real view of **YOUR** credit status. Are **YOU** noticing a pattern here? Yes... this is about **YOU**!

YOU purchased the book, **YOU** will do the work and **YOU** will reap the rewards of **YOUR** hard work. Let's get started!

Session 1 (Mini Session)

What Drives You?

The first step to true enlightenment begins with self awareness. Think about this... you manage your financial decisions; you drive your financial transactions, which in turn drive your credit status. What do those financial decisions say about you? I am of the belief that everything is done for a reason. That reason may be unclear to you when you're doing it, but if you take time to analyze your actions, you will uncover the true motivation behind each action. Napoleon Hill said, "If you do not conquer self, you will be conquered by self". You must define what drives your financial decisions before you can conquer your issues with credit management. Awareness of your actions leads to responsibility in financial management. Acknowledging the internal and external factors that drive financial decisions is a recurring issue amongst many of my clients and people who attend my seminars. I am also constantly amazed at the amount of people who don't seem to know the difference between wants and needs.

I am in the process of completing a financial management program that focuses on managing finances for success that is unlike any other financial program I've ever seen or heard of. The program is called; The 360 Degree Wealth Builder's Plan. Between the research for that project, my personal experiences and information from clients, I have come to realize that financial decisions are often made without any thought or reasoning. And for most of us, we have no one to blame but ourselves. I am also aware that

that there are some financial situations that happen outside your realm of control.

One of the services that my firm offers is free financial seminars for high school seniors preparing for college. After one of our seminars, a young lady approached me and asked if she could make an appointment to see me. She stated that she was 17 years old, planned to go to college to be a lawyer and knew that she would have to get loans to do so. This young lady had quite a distressed look on her face. I immediately recognized that look as one of a young person who wanted to shift the course of their life but did not know how to do it. That look was so familiar because it was the same look I had when I was a high school senior with no idea how I would get the money for college. I responded that there were hundreds of student loans out there and she should sit down with her parents and pick the one that's best for her particular situation. I turned to respond to another person, confident that the standard advice I'd just given her would suffice.

The distressed young lady politely tapped me on my shoulder and said, "Excuse me; I'm aware that there are loans available, but my situation is different". She went on to tell me that she'd just recently applied for a college loan and was denied due to her poor credit history. She noted that she was quite shocked because she had never applied for any credit. She later learned that her credit history was incredibly damaged because her mother had been using the young lady's name and social security number to get credit cards, apartments and various other types of credit since the young lady was 13 years old. She went on to say that her mother had defaulted on nearly all of the credit accounts and had been evicted from two residents in the last five years. This brave young person was clearly fighting back tears while she was explaining her unfortunate situation, but once she finished, the tears began to flow. This was a classic case of someone being taken advantage of... and by her mother, of all people. A situation completely out of her control.

Although I was quite sympathetic to her horrendous circumstances, I knew that standing around having a pity party wouldn't get her where she needed to be in less than a year. I pulled the young lady to the side, looked her sternly in the eyes and said, my heart goes out to you because you're in a situation that you did not put yourself in, we both know that. But after all is said and done **YOU** have to get yourself out of it, and you can, but I will help you if you're willing to do the work. She agreed and less than a week later, my team began working on her situation. Over the course of several meetings, my team and I were impressed by how dedicated this young lady was to turning her circumstances around. She may have started at a deficit but she had steely determination in her eyes and I knew that she would not give up until she was walking across that stage with her law degree in hand. Because of her determination and dedication, I was excited to help her! Who knows... we may have helped one of the future Supreme Court Justices of the United States of America.

I enjoy helping people educate themselves about their financial options, but my first criterion is; "you have to want to help yourself more than I want to help you". No matter what your situation, you must first acknowledge the factors that drive you to manage your finances as you currently do. Identify any internal and external factors that support those decisions, which requires making difficult decisions and sometimes even breaking destructive financial relationships. What do I mean by destructive financial relationships? Destructive financial relationships consists of any relationship that encourages or supports poor financial habits that do not contribute to your positive financial goals. Many of these relationships develop so naturally that they often go unnoticed until you get into real financial trouble. Once you've identified these relationships, you should then ask yourself the tough questions. If your friends/children/relatives/co-worker borrow money from you and never pays it back, why do you continue lending it? If you always pay your bills late and end up paying hundreds of dollars a month in late fees, why do you continue being late? If you're drowning in credit card debt but continue purchasing unnecessary items via credit, why are you choosing to sink deeper in debt? This process may be a bit overwhelming to you right now, but it will prove to be a lifesaver for your personal and financial well-being. I just have one question for you... are you really ready to change your life?

Homework (Session 1)

You should be driven by needs then wants. Do you know the difference between wants and needs?

Complete the homework for Session 1 in your workbook or e-book.

Session 2

My First Love

What drives us to manage or miss-manage our finances? That question has as many answers as there are people on this planet. Life has taught me that money has an equally strong emotional, psychological and social dimension as it does economic. If we were all strictly rational thinkers, we would always make wise financial decisions and would never be in debt. Many of our financial choices have nothing to do with necessity and more to do with our financial mentality. I am a facts and figures guy by trade, but I understand the desire for certain luxuries; the nice car, the five thousand square foot home, the international travel and so forth. I also know the "true cost" of those luxuries if they are not secured wisely. I can speak to this subject because I have been on just about every level of the financial ladder. When I was at the lower rung of that ladder, I desperately wanted many of those luxuries and worked hard to be able to afford them. Once I was able to afford those luxury items, they weren't as important to me.... my priorities shifted. That's when I learned that "things" cannot make you happy or fulfilled.

I have also learned, with age and wisdom, that not everything is black or white; there are shades of gray in almost every circumstance. The credit process, however, is the exception to that rule. No matter what the circumstance, your credit score is essentially seen as good or bad. Although lenders can view your detailed credit history via your credit report, they primarily make the decision to extend or deny credit based on your credit score. That is why it is extremely important to manage your finances and credit wisely. It is equally important to understand credit.

Credit was initially offered as a tool for financial management. One could purchase large ticket items; home, car, heavy equipment etc, over a specified amount of time for a nominal fee above the purchase price. At least that's how it started. The financial industry has taken some interesting turns over the years, some of which have been in our favor, some have not. Be that as it may, I still get a rush from working in the financial industry. Let me rephrase that, I love the infinite possibilities that the financial industry offers. The world revolves around commerce in one way or another and credit is just one form of it. The credit process, as we know it, has been around for as long as I can remember but wasn't always the standard operating procedure. My grandmother's generation did not use or abuse their finances the way that my generation did.

My grandmother Drucille's motto was, "if you don't have the cash then you probably don't need it." She often told me about the "good old days" when her parents purchased everything with cash. My grandmother was raised during the great Depression and she often bragged that they never went hungry because her parents farmed and used the barter system for all their needs. She kept those principles close to her heart as she grew older and was one of the best savers I had ever known. She did, of course, purchase big ticket items (home and car) on what she called "installment plans" but always felt that purchasing non-essential items on credit was dangerous. Whenever she needed to purchase something, she would simply save the money and eventually purchase it. Isn't it interesting that, on average, we make more money than our grandparents, but they managed to save more than we save and was even able to "find" money for emergencies?

My grandmother worked as a school matron (or janitor) most of her life. I remember walking to the school where she worked many days and helping her clean up after I left school, just to hear her stories. She was one of those old school grandmothers who always said she had no money and was barely making it, however... that all changed when one of the relatives needed some emergency money. My grandmother would try to collect the money needed from other relatives, but if that didn't work, she would start fussing about how we needed to help one another, as she casually walked to her bedroom. She would close the door slowly, as she continued fussing and within 10 minutes, reappear with the full amount of money that the relative needed. I always found it amazing that just 30 minutes earlier she didn't have the money but always seemed to miraculously "find" the money. My grandma was the first person to teach me the value of money and most importantly saving money. Grandma lost her battle with cancer in 2002 and I miss her dearly, but I will never forget the many lessons that she taught me about life and finance.

I can remember trying to follow my grandmother's "cash only" motto at a very early age. I was also like my grandmother in that I never wanted to depend on anyone for money and I hated being indebted to anyone. My attitude had a lot to do with where I was born and raised. I was born in Saint Louis Missouri and spent my early childhood in the Pruitt Igo projects. Pruitt Igo was the first housing project erected by the federal government. Ever wonder why they were called projects...because that's what they were, a project, test or experiment. The government built the high rises as a social/housing project and we were part of the first group of residents. We lived in the Pruitt Igo projects for a short while, along with other relatives. I remember asking a male relative for money one day and him turning to me and saying, "Boy, you ask for money everyday. You need to go get you a job so you can keep some money in your pocket and get out of these projects". He chuckled and walked away, but that statement lingered with me for days. I saw a job as a way to always "keep money in my pocket" and change my social status... so I got a job at the age of ten. I wish I could tell you that I began working at ten years old because I had to buy my own clothes or because I needed to help my poor, destitute family pay the bills. That would be a great tearjerker for this book but it would be untrue. The truth is - I began working so early, because I have always loved having money. It's true... my very first love was money.

I secured a job as a newspaper carrier at the age of ten. This was circa1972 and at that time the newspaper route supervisor gave new carriers all of the supplies they needed for their first week (i.e.: rubber bands, newspaper bag, plastic sleeves, etc) and deducted the money owed out of your first paycheck. I had a BIG problem with that plan. What they didn't know was, by age ten; I had already been robbed twice: once for my bike and once for my shoes, so I didn't like the idea of having my property taken without my permission. I informed the route supervisor that I did not want any money taken out of my check and I immediately began looking for ways to pay for the supplies on my own. I delivered my newspapers the first day and found that I had three papers left after I finished my paper route. I took the three remaining newspapers to school and sold them to some teachers in the teachers lounge for 50 cents instead of the required 25 cents. That's when I began honing my sales skills. I told them that they could get the newspaper cheaper; however, I offered great customer service and at-school delivery and that was worth an extra 25 cents.

The following day, I had more newspapers left after my deliveries. I also took some of the money from the previous day and purchased several additional newspapers. Back then, we used to have stand-alone metal boxes that contained a large stack of newspapers. One would simply put the required quarter in and remove ONE newspaper. I'm sure you know where this is going... I put my quarter in the newspaper box and withdrew several papers instead of one. I know that this wasn't the right thing to do and I'm not recommending that anyone follow in my footsteps, I'm just telling you what I did at the time. I took the newspapers that were left from my route and the papers that I'd gotten from the newspaper dispenser to school and sold them to teachers and administrators. I followed suit for the remainder of the week and by the end of the week I had collected the required money to pay my route supervisor for the supplies. When I got my first paycheck, it didn't have any money deducted and I was happy.

I've always had an affinity for finance; it's as natural to me as breathing. In fact, my fascination with finance actually started at a very young age. I can clearly remember going on treasure hunts in search of loose change as early as six years old. It didn't matter whether it was pennies, nickels, quarters or dimes; as long as it was money I was happy. This was, of course, before I learned the value of paper money versus coins. I searched under couch pillows, in cupboards, drawers, under beds, just about anywhere that I had found money previously or where I thought money may be hiding. If I had the same habits as a child today I would be diagnosed with a mild form of OCD, because it was a true obsession for me.

I can remember getting one of the best birthday presents of my young life, a brand new role of quarters. I got the roll of quarters for my sixth birthday and thought I had hit the jackpot! I remember running to my room, holding the roll of quarters high over my bed and shaking them out onto my bed. The glistening silver quarters were so bright and shiny; all I could do was stare at them. You would have thought that I was looking at flawless diamonds instead of $10 in quarters. My prize possession at the time was my pink ceramic piggy bank which contained the priceless treasure that I'd saved, or so my six year old mind imagined. I would often lie on my bed and stare at the piggy bank, with its astonishingly glossy exterior, contented smile and bloated belly just waiting to be filled with the priceless silver and copper coins. I fantasized about depositing coins into the piggy bank so much, that I actually heard coins dropping in my dreams.

Filling that piggy bank was a constant source of concern for me. I wondered what would happen when I filled the piggy bank completely. Would it burst under the weight of the millions of dollars worth of coins that it contained? Would I have to buy another piggy bank? What if I never got enough money to fill it? Would that mean that the kids at school were right; that I was just a poor fat welfare kid? As long as I had my millions in the piggy bank, I didn't care what they said. After I deposited the quarters into the piggy bank I remember taking great pride in lifting it and noting how heavy it had suddenly become. The heavier the piggy bank got the wider my six year old smile grew. I was old enough to reason that the heavier weight obviously meant that I was getting richer. And being rich meant that I was somebody special.

One of the biggest heartbreaks of my life happened a few months later when I came home and found my precious pink piggy bank lying on the floor of my room shattered into hundreds of pieces. Jagged pieces of glossy pink and dull gray ceramic were randomly strewn on the floor near the bottom of my bed. It looked like the piggy bank had exploded! Worst of all, there was only a few scattered pennies amongst the shattered pieces of ceramic; absolutely no shiny silver could be seen. When I realized that I was looking at my valued piggy bank, I began to scream; Oh my God, Oh my God, Grandma, somebody, come in here quick! I kneeled down to see if any of the silver coins were hiding under the scattered pieces of ceramic. I began sifting through the wreckage, pricking my fingers on the jagged pieces in hopes of finding my precious coins. Maybe the quarters had miraculously rolled under the bed or behind the drawer when the piggy bank was shattered. My six year old mind was rationalizing and panicking at the same time.

I frantically looked under the bed and found nothing. I searched the nearby dresser, looked under the rug, and moved the box that contained my toys; still nothing. That was it! It finally registered that the money was gone. I ran towards the kitchen and yelled, "all my money is gone; all my money is gone". I lead my grandmother into my room and showed her the scene of the crime. She looked at the shattered mess and said, it looks like it fell off your dresser honey. But where are my quarters, I replied with tears streaming down my face, I had millions of dollars in there. Well baby, why didn't you put your money in a safe place, she responded? The question stunned me. I looked at her in confusion wondering, "Was she actually blaming me for this"? Don't worry about it sweetie; she said quietly,

I'll take care of it. Come on in the kitchen and get some cake.

Even my grandmother's delicious lemon pound cake couldn't make the nightmare go away. All I could do was cry and eat cake, cry and eat cake. I was almost 13 years old before I found out that a (former) family friend had broken my piggy bank and stolen the money. The thief must have gotten into my room when no one was looking and committed the heinous crime. That was a pretty hard lesson to learn at such a young age, but as we know, we don't get to learn "life lessons" at our convenience. Since then, I have always been cautious about where I keep my money and who gets access to it.

After doing a large amount of soul searching to find out what "makes me tick", I realized that I didn't just house my coins in that piggy bank. Within the belly of that pink piggy bank laid my hopes for acceptance, a better life and all of the luxuries that I thought other kids had on a daily basis. A happy, loving two parent household, two parents who loved and protected me, a pet (preferably a dog), all of the latest toys that were advertised on TV, lots of friends who never called me fat or poor and most importantly all of the desserts that I could eat anytime I wanted them. It's interesting how you look at wants and needs as a kid, the line blurs rather constantly. My home life wasn't bad in comparison to some other kids; in fact, all of my **"needs"** were being met one way or another. We were by no means rich, but I certainly ate everyday, had clean clothes and got a few of those **"wants"** along the way. But in my adolescent heart there was a big hole and the treasure in that piggy bank helped me fill it. The piggy bank was symbolic of my desire to change the status of my day to day life and have people view me differently. My journey of self discovery began the day that I realized that fact.

I've met many people over the course of my career who, as adults, are still in search of that "thing" that will fill the emotional holes in their lives. Emotional fulfillment is a journey that some people are on for a short while, some take a bit longer on the journey and there are some people who leave this earth without ever finding that source of fulfillment. If you're asking what this has to do with managing your finances, I say... absolutely everything. As I stated earlier, there is a reason for every action. Your relationship to financial management generally has some type of emotional element tied to it. Some of those elements may be positive; however, some drive you to emotional spending and poor financial choices, which impacts your credit negatively. This session is all about soul-searching! I would like for you to take some time to pinpoint those things that are really important to you. In that soul searching, you should find some of the answers that you are chasing. Look beyond your status, image, environment and all of your purchased possessions. It's great to have all of that but honestly, does any of that fulfill you emotionally?

It's difficult for anyone to feel happy or fulfilled if they have a mountain of debt and bad credit weighing them down. I know what it's like to have more bills than income, to want more for your family but have no way to give it to them, to get those "collection agency" calls in the morning and at night. When I was getting the collection calls, I was so broke that I couldn't even afford caller ID so I couldn't avoid them. Many of us get into these situations because we don't fully understand ourselves or the credit process. We began participating in the financial process before we fully understand it. Most of us are introduced to credit at around age 18. Whether it's due to college expenses, credit cards, securing a residence, purchasing a car or some other expense, this is generally the time when most people begin stretching their financial wings. However, if you haven't taken the time to first identify what drives your financial decisions, you will never be able to spread your financial wings and soar. This book is your first step towards that self awareness. My greatest hope is that through these sessions and the homework, you will get the information you need in order to make the best financial decisions for you, internally and externally.

Homework (Session 2)

It's time to get to know YOU!

Complete the homework for Session 2 in your workbook or e-book.

Session 3

What is Credit?

I define credit as; an agreement that grants electronic money or real goods for a specified time period to be repaid by agreement of the borrower and lender. But... have you ever thought about what credit really is? You are asking an anonymous entity to make a large sum of virtual money available to you for whatever reason. This anonymous entity either grants or denies your request for the virtual money based on a number that specifies whether you will pay them back or default on your repayment agreement. It is incredible that the credit process takes place in so many areas of the unknown. What was once a simple process of allowing merchants to pay for product in "installments" has become this behemoth system that we know today as the credit system?

I generally begin my financial seminars with the following question: "by a show of hands, how many people are happy with their knowledge of credit and the credit process"? This question always evokes a collective groan from the audience, very few hands raised and every once in a while, a few expletives whispered throughout the crowd.

When I ask the same question during one-on-one credit classes, I generally receive one of three responses:

a. They roll their eyes in annoyance.

b. They begin making excuses for past financial mistakes.

c. They acknowledge that they are unaware, don't care to be aware, and simply want their credit "fixed"

I don't blame people for wanting to avoid the mess of untangling credit issues; it's not a fun thing to do. If I could, I would wave a magic credit repair wand over all of my client's credit issues and make the issues disappear. And before you ask, no...I haven't been visiting the liquor cabinet. I just want you to know that I sympathize with your credit situation. Since I don't currently own any such wand, we should start this session on a realistic note: there is no such thing as instant credit repair. There is no such service, company or organization that can legally make your factual credit entries disappear from your credit history... period. There is repair of inaccurate credit entries and improvement of negative credit entries; however, both of them take time and work. You must educate yourself about the process and take the necessary steps to improve, repair and maintain your credit. This book is designed to help you through the process.

Credit improvement and maintenance are offered as a service to all of my clients. This is in addition; however, to the other services we are providing such as wealth management (investments, retirement portfolio) real estate services, consulting and property management. I am blessed to have some rather wealthy clients; however, no matter how much money, properties or investments I am managing for them, I do not promise any miracles or unrealistic credit goals. I simply work with them to improve and maintain their credit. Those promises of instant credit repair are false whether you make ten thousand dollars a year or ten million, no matter what you see advertised. I'm sure that you've seen advertisements for various companies that offer unrealistic credit repair services such as 7 day credit repair. I sometimes see signs on the side of the road scribbled in magic marker advertising someone's ability to remove negative credit entries from one's credit history instantly... for some nominal fee of course.

I'm no Doubting Thomas, but as I stated earlier, I am, at my core, a facts and figures man and I have yet to encounter a company that can deliver on a promise to legally wipe your credit history clean or repair bad credit within a short amount of time. Given all of the external factors involved in the process; time being the main one, it is virtually impossible to do instantly. I must admit that I am not aware of EVERY service in the universe so there may be a company somewhere out there that can deliver on promises of repair. I can't personally attest to knowing any. Now that we have established our place of reality, let's dig in.

The credit process...

In order for you to fully understand what you'll need to do to improve your credit rating, you must fully understand how the credit process works. One goes through the credit process in order to be granted credit. The definition for the word credit, as a financial reference, varies depending on the source. Dictionary.com defines credit as:

2b) an amount or sum placed at a person's disposal by a bank

2c) the provision of money, goods, or services with the expectation of future payment; also: money, goods, or services so provided

3b) financial or commercial trustworthiness

Look at some of the key words used to define credit:

- ✓ *Future Payment*
- ✓ *Provision*
- ✓ *Trustworthiness*
- ✓ *Expectation*

These words are at the core of the credit process. In their own way, they explain why credit is extended or denied. I would venture to add one more key word to that list, one that is used by lenders more than any of the other words when issuing or denying credit. That word is:

✓ ***Perception***

Half Full?

↑ ↓

Half Empty?

Perception is defined as a person's view of a situation, based on their own beliefs, and it plays a major role when the potential lender is looking at your credit history and deciding your credit worthiness, even though it should not be a factor. Lenders are supposed to base their decision to grant or deny credit on a person's credit history, primarily; to identify your intent to repay a debt. The Equal Credit Opportunity Act requires creditors to apply credit standards in a fair manner, so that all consumers are given an equal chance to obtain credit. Furthermore, lenders are not supposed to discriminate on the basis of sex, marital status, race, religion, national origin, age or income from assistance programs under the Consumer Protection Act. Although lenders are required to abide by a fixed set of rules, the reality is that some lenders do not follow these rules. Be that as it may, the primary judgment regarding your ability to repay a debt is gleaned from your credit history. That is why it is so important to manage your credit carefully so that the perception is always based on factual information.

I was a loan officer for a major bank for many years, and was often verbally assaulted when I could not approve a loan due to someone's credit history. That is why it is important that you understand how the credit process works. Lenders don't know you personally, so don't take the process personally. You are a few sheets of facts and figures, where their lending process is concerned. Especially now, since much of the credit process is done electronically. It isn't the lender's job to help you straighten out issues on your credit report; it is your job to know what is on your credit report long before you ever go to the lender. If your credit history shows you've been late on your car payment for two months, the lender's perception is that you pay your bills late... period. The truth could be that the finance company moved two months before you were notified of the new address. You may have been sending your payments to the old address on time but they weren't forwarded to the new address. That is a legitimate reason for the late payments but the lender still cannot base their decision on that information. If your credit history shows that you defaulted on a school loan, the lender's perception is that you are not responsible with long-term financial responsibilities and you are likely to default on their loan as well...period. The facts could be that you are paying your school loan on time but there was a student in your class who has the same first, middle and last name as yours and all of your loan payments have been posted to their account for the past six months. Be that as it may, a lender cannot base their decision on that information.

If you apply for credit and have negative entries on your credit history, lenders will probably listen to your story, sympathize with you and they may even give you some tips on how to rectify the situation, but what they probably won't do is approve you for more credit. Again, don't make the mistake of going into the credit process and taking it personally. Lenders want to extend credit to you, that is how they keep their doors open; however, they can only make decisions based on the information that is posted in your credit history. What you say verbally, via email, text message or any other method has no bearing on that bottom line credit information and credit score.

Homework (Session 3)

Let's see if you were really paying attention.

Complete the homework for Session 3 in your workbook or e-book.

A Personal Credit Crisis

Just as we have evolved as human beings, the nature, use and concept of credit has evolved. I am a mature adult of 45 and have never known an American economic society that didn't revolve around the credit system. Throughout history, money and credit have evolved along with the social and psychological changes in our attitude towards what we value. Our actions speak much louder than our words when it comes to how we value money and credit.

I came of age during the early 1980s, the era of Reaganomics, and I fully embodied the "me" generation that was prevalent during that time. I was that dude in high school who wore a suit to school everyday, carried a brief case and wore my premium quality leather driving gloves while driving my 1975 Deuce and while in school. You couldn't tell me I wasn't the man. I went to Sumner High School, which was outside my neighborhood school district. Since I didn't live in the same neighborhood as most of my classmates, many of them thought that I was from a privileged up-bringing because I dressed well, had a car at 16 and seemed to always have money. What they didn't know was; I worked up to 35 hours per week at nights and on weekends, bought my car out of a junkyard, fixed and painted it myself and I lived in "the hood". I worked at a large grocery store chain called Nationals in St. Louis and spent most of my money on White Castles hamburgers, Imo's pizza, girls and clothes. It was important to me that I was the best dressed person at school or, at minimum, in the top three. They used to call it being "fly" back then and I tried to be the most fly dude in school everyday! Check me out...

Brian, circa 1981, with the Classic 80's "one hand in the pocket" pose.

You weren't anybody if you couldn't keep up with the latest styles and fads. Looking back, I realize that the value of my money was directly related to how many clothes I could buy, dates I could go on and how much gas I could put into my car.

I dressed well, for the time, but it wasn't until my freshman year of college that I found my personal style... or so I thought. I clearly remember the fall day in 1984 that I saw a show called Miami Vice. I was mesmerized by the coolness of the cars, flash of the clothes and beauty of the women. I knew right away that I wanted the Miami Vice lifestyle, or at minimum, the perception of that lifestyle. I already had a nice car, I just had to get the look in order to attain the most important part... the women. I decided to put my own signature spin on the Miami Vice look by mixing Crockett and Tubbs' signature styles. I decided to wear the Miami Vice type jacket, a dress shirt and skinny tie. But I would switch it up by wearing white dress pants and shoes instead of the linen pants and loafer styled shoes. The best part was I already had everything I needed for the ensemble except the white pants and white shoes.

This was 1984 so the most popular pants worn then were called baggies. They were dress pants that were very similar to M.C. Hammer's genie pants, but a bit more form fitted. I'm sure this sounds like an incredible fashion mistake to you young readers, but all of the 40 plus readers can surely remember seeing or wearing baggies. I imagined myself in the brand new white baggie pants with the razor sharp crease, freshly pressed dress shirt, my signature skinny tie, double breasted dress jacket, and brand new white pointy dress shoes with the laces. I also imagined the reaction I would receive when I arrived on campus in that outfit. I envisioned a group of beautiful girls whispering amongst themselves as I got out of the car; wow, who is that, is he a movie star or something, he sure is fly; I wonder if I could be his girl. Sufficed to say that the imaginary scene went as far as me having to break up a catfight between the girls regarding who would get to be with me.

With that very vivid scenario playing in my head, I decided that nothing would deter me from obtaining that look. The fact that those pants and shoes would require half my paycheck and I would be short on food money for a week meant nothing to me. The value of that outfit even outweighed my need for food. As soon as I got paid that Friday, I went to the local mall to get those pants and shoes. I was incredibly disappointed to find that I didn't have enough money to buy both the pants and shoes; I was $15 dollars short. Buying one or the wasn't an option for me. I had to have the outfit that I had envisioned in order to get the girls that I had envisioned.

As I stood there trying to figure out where I could get $15, the guy behind the counter said; my man, you look like you want that outfit pretty bad. I responded with a very suspicious nod. Are you a college student? Yes, I responded, with even more suspicion. "This is what I'll do for you my man", he said, you can open a credit account and get the clothes right now. I stood there thinking about accepting the offer, but also thought about my grandmother's advice, "if you don't have the cash you probably don't need it". I'd been relatively wise with my money up until that point and I didn't want to mess that up. I stood there for what seemed like 30 minutes, just staring at the brand new white pants and shoes, contemplating my next move. Although I didn't plan to open a credit account that day, the vision of those beautiful girls was much louder than my grandmother's sage advice. I opened the credit account and got the clothes. Only later did I find out that the credit account carried an interest rate of over 25% and fees that totaled $35 per month, although I had excellent credit and had never been late on any bills.

Even more disappointing than that was the reality of the outfit itself. Although I made quite a statement when I wore the outfit, the "beautiful girls whispering" scenario never became a reality, therefore, my Miami Vice fashion phase was very short lived. I did, however, get a date with one girl that I'd been pursuing, so it did serve its purpose. See for yourself...

Brian, circa 1984. Crockett and Tubbs had nothing on me! My friends are probably posting this on YouTube as we speak.

Although my Miami Vice phase was very short lived, the credit account that I opened caused me a lot of headache before I finally closed it. Looking back, there were three main things that drove my need to open that account:

1. **Emotions** *(popularity, acceptance, girls)*
2. **Fad/Fashion** *(had to have the latest and greatest)*
3. **Consumer Driven Market** *(vendor capitalized on my "I want it now" consumer mentality by offering easy access to credit)*

The value of my hard-earned money and good credit did not compare to the value that I placed on getting that outfit.

By my junior year in college I had matured considerably. I went back to my grandmother's sage advice, as well as making wiser financial decisions. As I drew closer to graduation, I realized that I would need good credit and some type of savings to help me move forward as an adult. I began saving as much money as possible, dressing like a regular college student (jeans and t-shirts) and I even got a more fuel efficient car; a 1978 metallic purple Volkswagen Beetle. Yes... I had a metallic purple Volkswagen Beetle, and I'm quite proud of it.

Brian and the Purple Bug

My financial mentality evolved from that of a reckless spender to a survivalist to its current state; a thriver! Luckily, I didn't have as much trial and error as some of my friends; I was wise enough to learn from my early mistakes.

At one point in history, the importance of your credit rating only affected big-ticket purchases; however, like most things, credit has evolved. Your credit history is now viewed by many potential employers as one of the criteria of employment. Yes... your credit history may affect your employment options! That is why you need to understand not only how credit works today, in addition, you should understand the evolution of the credit process in a historical context. Understanding the history of U.S. credit, finance and consumerism is essential to understanding how the credit process has evolved over the years and what drove the major changes. This historical information will offer a better understanding of some key triggers that drive change within our current economy today as well.

Homework (Session 4)

How will you change your mentality from a survivor to a thriver!

Complete the homework for Session 4 in your workbook or e-book.

The Evolution of Credit

. . . it was hardly an exaggeration to say that the American standard of living was bought on the installment plan.
-Daniel Boorstin, historian

Although we can trace various forms of credit to their origins over the course of human evolution, it is equally important to identify the societal and psychological changes that accompanied the evolving credit process. Let's travel back in time for a U.S. history lesson in commerce, credit and consumerism.

Barter vs. Banker

Although some form of credit has always been in use in America; credit has been the predominate form of economic transactions in American society for the last 60 years. Before currency was exchanged for goods and services, the barter system was used as the primary means of exchange. A barter system is a system of trade for goods and services where one form of goods or services is traded for another form of goods or services. The earliest recorded banking/barter establishments were royal temples, palaces and supply houses in Mesopotamia and Egypt. These facilities were used to store grain and other precious commodities of the day because these particular facilities offered the security of royal guards. People had to make a deposit of some sort of commodity and they would be issued a receipt. They would use this receipt to trade their goods with other parties instead of having the actual goods in hand. Both parties would take the receipts to the facility where the goods were being stored and receive the product for the receipt. In addition to bartering, this was an early, very primitive form of banking. As this practice grew in popularity, private banking houses began to appear. *(These banking houses are mentioned in the Babylonian Code of Hammurabi - c1760BC)*

Early American Trade

A culture of consumption has almost always been prevalent in America. The puritanical Victorians utilized the barter system but approved of piano purchases on credit because the piano was a primary source of social entertainment. It didn't take much to jump from justification of luxury items for social enjoyment to purchasing luxury items on a whim. Sixteenth century Americans relied on the barter system as a primary system of trade from the time that the Pilgrims happened upon America and began settling in the Native American's back yard (1620 AD approx). The barter system was also an important social function in early American society. It played a large role in keeping the community connected as it was often the only time neighbors interacted outside religious ceremonies. The barter system reigned supreme for many years; however, as societal norms began to shift, so did the premise of the barter system.

For example, if one settler had a basket of tomatoes but wanted a chicken, they would find a settler who had a chicken and wanted to trade for the tomatoes. No contract, no 30 day return policy, just a simple hand to hand trade. Problems arose with this system however. The settler with the tomatoes would have to search until they found someone who had a chicken AND needed tomatoes AND was willing to trade for the chicken. That proved to be quite troublesome for many a settler. Remember that settlements during this period were densely populated with the next closest settlement generally being too far to walk, especially carrying a basket of tomatoes. So the settler with the tomatoes had a dilemma; they needed to find someone who:

a) needed tomatoes
b) had a chicken to trade
c) wanted to trade the chicken for the tomatoes
d) was in close proximity
e) felt that the chicken for tomatoes trade was fair

or

f) NO DEAL!

The number of delimiting factors made the barter process quite complicated at times. The barter system eventually turned to a system of trade for symbolic forms of money, initially titled "trade bills", which were regulated by banks.

And Banking Begins

The first North American bank was established after the American Revolution (c1782): The Bank of North America. Several banks followed in various states including different forms of currency in each individual state. The dollar was established shortly thereafter as the new national currency and was adopted by each state as the official form of currency. The original dollar was backed by gold and silver and credit was extended by store owners. From the late 1700s, credit was available to the average patron; however lenders only offered credit to their neighbors or people they knew. Most patrons and store owners were neighbors so they felt comfortable executing a general "promise to pay" agreement for goods and services. This era was, however, the end of credit as a means for securing goods needed to survive or for vocation. It is during this time that we slowly began utilizing credit to feed our need for luxuries. Let's look at how lifestyle played a part in the cash to credit shift in the early 19th century.

The "Hard" Old Days

The early to mid 1800s were a time of hard labor and very few creature comforts. Men, women and children spent the majority of their time working, often working from sun up to sun down. I imagine that they were too tired to walk the numerous miles it took to visit neighbors by the end of a long work day. The strict lifestyle of work and not much else is evident in the fact that the most popular thing to do for recreation during that time was read the bible.

The Rapidly Changing Society

The late 1800s brought about big changes for the work weary American. Railroads and roads were expanding so travel was more of an option. Communication options increased as the telegraph system expanded and the first transatlantic cable connected Europe and North America. And most importantly the big societal shift from agricultural to industrial began in the late 1800s. By the end of the 19th century, the United States was well on its way to becoming one of the world's leading industrial economies.

Large-scale factory production and falling transportation costs had brought an astonishing variety of new products onto the market. Consumerism was on the rise during this time because new products began to catch the eye of "regular people" who worked at good paying jobs. Their income began to afford more additional luxury items and not just the bare necessities. They were able to afford some of the less expensive items such as new clothes, shoes, radios; however, many of the new products (i.e.: sewing machines, stoves, farm equipment) were unattainable to them due to the high price tag. Since large amounts of credit weren't available to the average person; they had four options for acquiring the funds needed:

1) Family Members
A family member or family members loaned the person the money required with a promise to repay, oftentimes without interest.

2) Local Retailers
Local retailers had personal connections with their customers in the late 19th century and began offering them product under an installment plan.

3) Pawnshops
Pawnshops were once a socially accepted option for securing money. People could take an item of value to the pawnshop (i.e.: jewelry, appliances, etc); the pawnshop owner would inspect the item and offer a certain amount of money to hold the item for a certain amount of time. The Pawnshop interest rates were often high, but if you default on a loan from a pawn shop you simply lose your merchandise.

4) Loan Sharks
Loan sharks offered large sums of money to anyone but attached a hefty interest rate to be repaid along with the original loan. You could receive a fate much worse than a negative credit entry if you defaulted on your loan from a loan shark ... I'll just leave it at that.

The "Installment" Era

In 1919 General Motors Acceptance Corporation (GMAC) became the first to make financing available to middle-income car buyers. Instead of having to come up with the entire purchase price, prospective car buyers needed only a down payment and an income that was big enough to cover monthly payments over the life of the loan. Before long, manufacturers of other "big ticket" items began to adopt the "installment credit" practice. They revolutionized the way big business viewed installment credit. Then came the 1920s!

The roaring 20s came in with a bang! There was mass production, highway construction, mass communication and the expansion of consumer financing. Assembly line production was developed to the point of perfection and America began to produce cars at a price that made car ownership affordable for the working class. Other household products became available that made home life easier and more luxurious. Electrical power grid, phone lines, and water and sewer systems helped to bring these products into more homes. This is also the time that purchases of luxury items on credit began increasing to the point where most all stores offered some sort of merit or installment based purchase plan. All these industrial and technological marvels were made available to Middle Americans through the rapidly expanding use of installment credit. The big shift in American consumerism came when advertising and mass media outlets (newspapers, magazines, radio) began flooding consumers with ads that helped them overcome their inhibitions about purchasing unessential product. The advertising industry definitely helped drive the atmosphere of luxury, decadence and prosperity.

Unfortunately, the prosperity was not shared evenly amongst all Americans. According to a study done by the Brookings Institute, in 1929 the top 0.1% of Americans had a combined income equal to the bottom 42%. That same 0.1% of Americans in 1929 controlled 34% of all savings, while 80% of Americans had no savings at all. This maldistribution of income between the "haves" and the "trying to haves" grew throughout the 1920's.

Nevertheless, consumers continued purchasing big-ticket luxury items to keep up with the demand of advertisements. By 1926, following World War 2, people thought it "un-American" to be thrifty. Consumption and consumerism fueled American's desire to have a more luxurious life and thrift fell by the wayside.

The Worst of Times

The booming automobile and fuel industry helped lead to one of the most prosperous times in America. When these two industries slowed down, so did the entire economy. Because the great prosperity of the 1920s wasn't balanced between different industries, when the industries that were driving the economic prosperity slowed down (automobile and fuel), the whole economy slowed, subsequently... all of American industry fell.

By the second half of the 1920s, concerns regarding consumerism and consumption focused almost exclusively on the extension of credit to the household. Consumer debt, while relatively stable over the preceding two decades, increased substantially during the 1920s. Installment selling reached its peak during 1925-1927 and after the 1920s, there was no turning back. Widespread use of consumer credit became an indispensable part of American economic life. But for the next 40 years it was still limited mainly to installment buying. The people who extended you the credit were the same ones who sold you the product you were buying.

Retail stores and oil companies were issuing credit cards during the 1920s, but they were single-party cards issued by merchants who saw them as a way to sell more goods and services. They offered cardholders a certain measure of convenience but very little flexibility. Department store cards weren't accepted by competitors, and unless they were issued by a national chain, they weren't much use when traveling.

Gasoline credit cards covered a wider market area, but they weren't accepted by competitors, nor were they much use if you needed something that wasn't sold at a gas station. The party stopped in America on Tuesday, October 19, 1929; Black Tuesday. The Great Depression began and lasted until the early 1940s.

Depression to Credit Card Boom

The bombing of Pearl Harbor took place on December 7, 1941. There were still a lot of problems going on at the time of the Pearl Harbor bombing. It was only after that when the US got involved with the war, producing new machinery, airplanes, ammunition, bombs, etc, that the nation became busy, and a lot of new jobs were available. It gave the illusion that we were doing better. The 1940s brought about a new innovation in the credit industry; credit cards. Credit cards as we know them today didn't take off until the 1960s, when financial innovation, improved technology, and changing consumer attitudes all converged. Financial innovation came in the form of a concept pioneered by Diners Club in 1949: the dual-party card.

Dual-party cards represented a major breakthrough because the card issuer wasn't actually providing the goods or services being purchased. Diners Club was not a restaurant chain or a food service company. It simply signed up hotels and restaurants to participate in its credit card plan, and it then issued cards to creditworthy people who were willing to pay a yearly fee for the convenience and status of having a card. When a cardholder charged a meal, the restaurant sent the bill to Diners Club, and Diners Club then paid the price of the meal, minus a small commission, directly to the restaurant's bank. Finally, Diners Club sent the cardholder a monthly statement (bill), and the cardholder sent Diners Club a check. But Diners Club was only a first step.

The innovation that ultimately put dual-party credit cards into so many wallets was the bank card. A bank card was a general-purpose card that consumers could use in a wide variety of situations. Franklin National Bank (Franklin Square, New York) introduced the first bank card program in 1951. A few years later, Bank of America launched BankAmericard (now Visa), and Chase Manhattan Bank followed with MasterCharge (now MasterCard). When they first came on the market, general purpose credit cards were slow to catch on. Large retailers with well-established credit card programs of their own were reluctant to participate in bank card programs, and attracting cardholders and merchants from outside an issuing bank's marketing area was problematic. Eventually, large retailers set aside their reluctance when they realized that general-purpose cards made it easier for customers to spend even more in their stores and targeted advertising eased the concern for consumers from outside an issuing bank. The way was cleared for the credit boom!

Hi-Tech to New Millennium

The end of the 20th century brought about some incredible technological inventions and advances. By the early to mid eighties technology had overcome the problem of distance regarding the use of credit cards. Improved telecommunications and better computers gave banks and merchants the tools to move information quickly and manage it more efficiently. One of the big changes in the financial industry began to take off in the 1980s; the debit card.

After a long period in which debit transactions grew slowly, debit transaction volume began to grow very rapidly in the mid-1990s. Although debit cards were in use during the 1980s, transaction volume was somewhat low. In the early 1990s debit card volume was more noticeable. Online debit represented about 60 percent of debit transactions in the early 1990s. The number of cards in circulation that have a debit function (either online or offline) has also grown rising from 130 million in 1985 to 287 million in 2002. It is clear that the late 1990s witnessed a major change in how consumers use their debit cards. Aggressive marketing on the part of banks helped familiarize debit cardholders with the card, as did the emergence of Visa and MasterCard's offline debit products, which opened up their credit card product to debit cardholders. By the late 1990s, cash began to fall by the wayside as the primary method of currency.

Quick exchanges of information were the key to making the whole system work. Today, a store owner halfway around the world is able to receive electronic approval from your credit card issuer, and if the card issuer says you're OK, that's all the merchant needs to know. The use of consumer credit has become a fixture of everyday life. In 2000, more than 70 percent of U.S. households had at least one general-purpose credit card (i.e.: MasterCard, Visa, or Discover). Thirty years earlier, in 1970, the number was only 16 percent.

Information moved at the speed of an electronic impulse in the late 20th century. Between 1998 and 2001, the number of U.S. households with Internet access nearly doubled, from 26 percent to 50.5 percent. More than 56 percent of U.S. households had a home computer. Close to 95 percent of U.S. households had telephone service, and more than 98 percent had at least one TV. The population had shifted from rural to urban areas, with 75 percent of the US population now residing in urban areas. The average work week had decreased from approximately 50 hours to roughly 40 hours and people continued to fill the remainder of their weekly with recreational activities. And the staple of the American status symbol, the automobile, had increased in numbers to 210 million by the end of the

20th century. All of this begs the question; are we approaching the end of "easy access credit", as we know it?

The Credit Crisis Cometh!

The sub-prime mortgage disaster had a domino affect on the national economy, which led to a full-blown credit crisis by late 2007. The credit crisis exposed ubiquitous weaknesses in financial industry regulations and the international financial system. Many US mortgages that have been issued within the last 5 years are subprime mortagages. Subprime means that there was little to no down payment made on the mortgages and many mortgages were given to people with low income and poor credit history. When US housing prices began to decline, mortgage delinquencies soared which resulted in a decline in capital for banks. This further resulted in massive credit tightening by government and federal agencies around the world. People began to fear that credit would not be readily available and they stopped buying as many goods and services. We then saw a sharp decline in the economy, which led to the Recession of 2008. It is not dissimilar to what happened during the Great Depression of the 30's and 40's. People who lost money when banks collapsed in the Great Depression began hoarding their money as well. They hid their money under their mattresses, in their back yards and anywhere else they felt was safer than banks. People are unwilling to spend their money because they don't know when they will get it back. Financial institutions are unwilling to loan money because they don't trust that they will be paid back.

The efforts made through the federal bail-outs were primarily an effort to restore trust in a system that people were very skeptical of more than anything. Our collective challenge is to recognize that there is not and will never be a shortage of currency (dollars and coins) as long as we continue doing the printing. We can throw billions of dollars at the problem but the house of debt that we've built is dangerously close to being blown down. So... what is the remedy to resolve the economic crisis? Former President Bush's $700 billion dollar bailout? President Obama's multi-billion dollar bailout? The expectation behind both bailouts was that the government would relieve the banks of the staggering burden of bad debts so that the banks would have enough trust to start offering credit again. But the banks were still slow to offer credit. Instead, the banks continued to tighten credit lines and reduce credit limits. Some of them even began buying other banks. The result was that credit still did not flow freely. Everyone who depended on borrowed money was being squeezed. When credit stops flowing, the money supply shrinks. The cascading effect puts the entire global economy at risk because the whole house of cards depends upon borrowed money.

As the system of credit dries up, the more fear is created, and the more banks and other institutions will treat credit as something to hide under the mattress. The apprehension of investors will be one of the biggest hurdles for credit markets in the coming years. Investors now view anything tied to mortgages with skepticism, and as a result, companies are having a harder time securing money to operate and grow their businesses. Mortgage companies are tightening lending standards and credit card companies are slashing credit limits, just when consumers need access to capital. The outlook is not all bleak though.

In addition to what many consider the resilience of the global economy, independent wealth funds have stocked trillions of dollars for investment and are prepared to make those funds available. The Federal Reserve is expected to keep cutting rates, the unemployment rate is slowly beginning to steady and economists expect the economy to rebound by the second quarter of 2010. The Treasury Department's move to stem the tide of foreclosures could also help. In other words, calm will be restored and recovery is coming. But don't expect the road to recovery to be perfectly smooth.

Homework (Session 5)

The poor and uneducated pay for everything... but knowledge is the universal game changer!

Complete the homework for Session 5 in your workbook or e-book.

Session 6

Cyber Credit

Imagine a world where the paper and coin form of currency is no longer accepted for goods and services. In fact, the only place you can see paper or coin currency is in The Smithsonian. Grandparents regale eager children with stories of the olden days... the early 2000s, when people would actually walk into stores, choose product and give people called cashiers a certain amount of cash and coins in order to make purchases. The children ooo and ahhh in disbelief at this strange world of old called the New Millennium. In the bold new futuristic world, the credit/debit card process as we know it no longer exists and all forms of trade are virtual. Does this sound like an episode of the Twilight Zone? Insert some flying cars, meals in pill form and robot servants and it would be Isaac Asimov's iRobot come to life.

Don't scoff at this futuristic scenario...it may not be long before you are faced with a similar reality. It may be a bit far fetched to believe that financial transactions will be initiated and powered by brain waves or sheer will of thought, but it isn't too far fetched to believe that a more realistic version of this virtual process will be in place within the next 5 to 7 years.

As you can probably tell, I am a big fan of futuristic TV shows and movies. When I was a kid, I enjoyed watching Star Trek and considered myself a Trekkie. I have since been informed, by disciples of the USS Enterprise, that simply watching the show does not classify me as a bonafide Trekkie and have been downgraded to average fan. I was fascinated by movies based around time travel as a late teen and I absolutely love movies like, The Matrix, and Minority Report which depict scenes of futuristic abilities that one can only imagine. I often wonder how writers conceive of the futuristic concepts in those movies. Is it possible that future generations will be able to navigate space, time and travel in order to visit various dimensions? Or will we one day be able to harness the full power of our brains and see far enough into the future to stop crimes before they happen?

The future holds infinite promise and I believe that we will see some of the more realistic technological developments brought to life within the next 5 to 10 years. As John Lennon wrote, "you may say I'm a dreamer, but I'm not the only one". I have no doubt that there are computer technicians, scientists and microphysicists currently working on this space-aged technology as you read this book. This futuristic financial concept seems pretty far fetched to some, but who would have ever imagined that we would be able to look at TV/movies, listen to music, send and receive messages, take pictures and much more all from your telephone? Just imagine what our grandparents and great grandparents would think if they saw some of the technology that we use today? It would blow their minds! The financial industry is also looking to transport credit and transaction processing to intergalactic heights. It generally takes a substantial amount of time to test and implement changes where money and credit are concerned because most people are cautious when it comes to trusting new technology with their livelihood. That is why many of the technological breakthroughs currently used within the financial industry were in the test market for over five years. So... put your imaginary neural processing helmet on and open your mind to the possibilities of the financial future... the way I see it.

I'm not clairvoyant and these are simply my personal predictions; however, I am a student of American history, trending and consumerism. I am wise enough to see three things obvious facts relating to finance and credit:

1) The credit process can't be reversed.

2) We definitely can't stay where we are.

3) We MUST continue the shift towards more technologically advanced and paperless forms of transactions.

We are already processing transactions with virtual currency, which we consider credit. So what's next? Virtual transactions without physical intervention of course. Virtual transactions without physical intervention...hmmm, let's just think about that. My trusty Webster.com defines the word virtual as: existing in essence or effect though not in actual fact. This definition still holds some scary connotations for some of the baby boomers (1946 - 1964) who are used to the comfort of knowing that their physical money is safely held by a bank. It also causes a small bit of concern for some of us X-Genners (1965 - 1983) who are still not 100% comfortable with the security of electronic transactions. Our fear of identity theft via cyber-thieves has not fully subsided. But the members of Generation Y (1982-2000) and The Millenials (2001 - future) will most likely embrace the new virtual processes because they have never known a world without virtual transactions and processes.

Your next question is probably... what's going to happen to the cash and coin currency system...where will our cash go? We may not be that far away from a world where cash follows the dinosaurs into extinction and very few transactions are conducted face to face. As more and more of us become comfortable with the security of electronic transactions, we begin to use and keep cash on-hand less and less. Given the history of our current form of currency, the new virtual process may just be a welcome change.

The currency that we utilize today is actually legal tender or a banknote, which means, it is simply a promissory note towards a debt owed. As quiet as it's kept, our currency has had somewhat of a checkered past since its inception. Currency was once backed by gold and silver bullion. When the American currency was actually backed or insured by something, cash truly was king. The switch from gold and silver backed currency happened in the early 1930s, around the time of the Great Depression. This was also around the time that the modern form of currency was introduced. Thus began our downward spiral of operating in a debt based financial system. This system of "credit backed by debt" that our financial world revolves around currently has us owing international bankers trillions of dollars in interest alone.

The dollar's worth has fluctuated over the last hundred plus years. With the current dollar being worth little more than the paper it's printed on, and with world markets refusing to honor the value of the dollar as it once did, we are looking at the imminent demise of U.S. cash as currency. Frankly speaking, I'm not sure whether that's a negative thing. The fact that the paper currency that we think of as having value is simply a note of debt that is backed by more debt should have brought about major concern amongst "we the people" long ago. Either way, cash seems to have been on a steady path towards extinction since the popularity of the debit card.

The daily use of the debit card is now the norm. The debit card offers much more convenience for day to day use as well as banking; however, this system does not offer fool-proof privacy or security against identity theft and fraud. This has resulted in the need for more security efficient electronic systems that protect user privacy and a built in system to reduce fraud. This too is driving the development of E-money with no physical interaction. It offers fewer hand-to-hand transactions and allows encryption of data being transferred. The major pitfall of e-money; however, is that although it offers a greater level of fraud and user protection, it also allows easier access into your everyday transactions via virtual methods.

E-Money 101

The current version of E-money transactions comes in three forms:

- Card not present purchases
- Face-to-face purchases
- Third party facilitators

Card not present transactions are overwhelmingly used via the internet. This includes purchasing items online, downloading music or even paying bills online. Any transaction where you have to enter your credit or debit card information on a website or in a system is a card not present transaction. The vendor is making a purchase but is not physically viewing your card for verification and you complete the transaction from the convenience of your own home...or wherever you are. This form of transaction is done completely virtually. I must note that online bill paying is gaining ground as a card not present transaction and is currently being used by a growing number of consumers.

Face-to-Face transactions are still the dominant form for purchasing items. These transactions require you to go to a physical location and complete your transaction by giving the merchant a credit card, debit card or cash. When using a credit or debit card, many vendors now check identification to verify that the information on the card matches. This is a minor form of fraud protection as it is visual.

The last form of e-money transactions are ***third party facilitated transactions***. These transactions are initiated by the consumer but processed or facilitated by a third party company, such as Pay Pal, to complete the financial transaction. Often, companies who do not want to house the expense of a full time accounting department or include electronic financial processes on their web site hire third party facilitated websites to complete financial transactions for them. These third party payment facilitated websites can direct you to the third party site to complete payment or they can process the payment through the vendor's website. Either way, the third party facilitator is handling the entire financial transaction. This transaction is similar to the "card not present" transaction, however, it is a bit more risky because you now have two databases that can potentially store your credit or debit card information in their systems.

How will this no-contact process work?

The no-contact purchase process will automatically deduct money from your bank account, of course, as well as contain your picture, in case the merchant requires visual identification. This process is currently being tested in a hand full of markets in the U.S. but is not widely used yet. Some of the current no-contact processes have "Pass" in the title, such as E-Pass, Quick-Pass or something similar, indicating that the user can simply wave a (RFID) card in front of the ID reader to complete their transactions and pass through. The cards will contain built-in electronic signatures, so you won't have to worry about that either. Currently, you have to sign up for programs that offer no-contact transactions, as you need to put a signature on file. In the future; however, I believe that the process will be simplified and you will no longer need to sign up for a special program, it will simply be issued to you via your bank. You won't have to put any kind of card in a machine, give it to the clerk or pull out any cash to complete your transaction. In fact, I predict that once this technology is perfected, widely used and the public trusts that it is 100% safe; we will then see the quick demise of cash.

Will this new technology be safe?

I must admit that my concerns regarding fraud and theft prohibit me from fully trusting this technology just yet. I have been a victim of credit fraud and am well aware of how easy it is for someone to steal your credit information and use it without recourse. I shudder to think what damage a thief could do with a no-contact process. We are in the early testing phase for some of the no contact technology but it is on its way, whether we're ready or not. I'm pleased that this technology is currently being tested in both the US and the UK. I have no doubt that they are putting measures in place to combat identity theft as best they can. By the time this technology is widely used, it may not be fool-proof but as long as it's 100% track able, I am on board.

Homework (Session 6)

You get a pass on homework for this session... but enjoy it!
We're heading into the deep end of credit.

Just relax and keep reading!

Session 7

Credit Reporting

You're probably like many of my clients who wonder how the credit process came from a system of simple promissory notes that contain a few lines of general information to national credit corporations housing up to ten years of your detailed financial information. It's simple; once the credit reporting process was widely accepted there was a need for someone to compile and manage the data. Someone met the demand and the rules around the process were established as a result. Like any other development, some rules and processes were put in place by design and some developed organically. Its sound rather simplistic - and you know what... it is.

Although everyone may not agree on the accuracy of the current credit reporting system, we all agree that some sort of vetting process is required. Answer this question; would you lend money to someone without knowing anything about them? You purchased this book; therefore you are obviously quite intelligent, so I will answer that for you...of course you wouldn't. What about that relative or friend who always borrows money but never pays it back or does not pay it back when they agree to pay it? Would you continue lending to them even though they have a history of never repaying or always pays late? Of course you wouldn't. It doesn't matter who that person is, you would either think twice about loaning to them or simply refuse to loan money to them. And don't act like you don't have a relative or friend who fits that description. You know the one who constantly borrows money, "until they get paid", but their payday never comes, where your money is concerned. We all know someone like that. And if you say that you don't know anybody like that...that person may just be you.

Lenders feel the same way. They want to know as much as possible about you before offering credit. It's simple evolution of the credit vetting process. In Session 4, we learned that the credit process evolved over time along with the shift in America's mentality in consumerism. As the process evolved, so did the need for personal and sensitive information. As the need for information grew, so did the need to protect that personal information. The more advanced the technology became, the better corporations became at offering information and protecting that information. Either way, it all results in the credit reporting system that we currently use today.

Why was the credit reporting process started?

The basic concept of credit reporting can be traced back as early as the 1860's. The early form of credit reporting functioned primarily to provide local merchants with a way to keep tabs on the people who traded and did business in their immediate area. The early credit reporting agencies were a group of banks and merchants who agreed to keep a list of individuals who were poor credit risks. Prior to the use of a list, merchants extended only a very small amount of credit, based on the lender's personal knowledge of the customer. It was a time consuming and inaccurate process to gather sufficient information on a credit applicant. The lender or bank would have to call each creditor listed on the credit application before they would decide to extend credit. Some information provided by the early credit bureaus included:

- Personal Info (i.e.: name, address, etc)
- Employment records
- Public Records
- Information from landlords

The general population became more mobile after World War I and several advances in technology helped credit reporting progress. As the population became more mobile the merchant base began to expand. The credit industry began to provide information on consumers that could be accessed electronically; thereby, offering information with no geographical restrictions. Along with the mobilization of consumers came the need for lenders, merchants and businesses to make faster decisions about credit-worthiness. The credit reporting process was soon centralized and streamlined to more closely reflect the basic process used today.

Today's credit reporting process includes highly sensitive and personal information for each individual. The expansion of available credit, especially credit cards, requires detailed credit reporting and monitoring options. Recent estimates indicate that there is somewhere around one billion credit cards in use in the U.S. There is also reportedly approximately two billion pieces of data entered monthly with the major credit bureaus managing millions of credit files. Can you imagine that, managing millions of files with thousands of pieces of information per file, sequentially?

The internet and it's ever evolving technologies have presented some challenges to the credit reporting process. The demand for quick access to consumer information has prompted the credit bureaus to offer consumer information and many of their services on-line. The major credit bureaus were somewhat reluctant to offer consumer information on-line due to the sensitive nature of the information and the ongoing threat of identity theft and consumer fraud. The challenge of protecting consumer information has been daunting as consumers become more technically savvy and fears of security breach and identity theft run rampant. However; the technological age was upon us and the national credit bureaus had to get past their technological reluctance. The national credit bureaus jumped on the technology band wagon and began offering consumer credit information and services online.

Although computers manage the data once it is entered into the system, human beings enter the initial data. And with anything that involves human beings, human error is a possibility, which is why most people have found at least one error on their credit report. Think about it, with all of the people in the United States of America with similar social security numbers or birth dates, it is highly likely to have an error on a credit report over the course of your life. You should not expect errors; however, the odds are high that you will find an error over the course of your life, if you are diligent about checking your credit report. A simple error, such as misspelled address or street or social security number on your credit report may match someone else's personal information. If that person's information finds its way onto your report and their credit information is included with yours, it leads to inaccurate information for you.

You obviously want to update erroneous information no matter how minor it is. The person being reporting on your credit file may have negative items on their report, which will affect your information AND SCORE. Negative information in your credit history reflects negatively on you, whether it is accurate or not. Either way erroneous information on your credit report is never a good thing. This book contains detailed information about repairing erroneous information on your credit report, but there is a lot more you should learn before that... so keep reading.

Homework (Session 7)

This starts your personalized plan!
Complete your homework THOROUGHLY.

Complete the homework for Session 7 in your workbook or e-book.

What is a Credit Bureau?

Ahh... the good old Credit Bureau. Never have two words created such an emotional reaction, built primarily on myths and false information. The myriad of myths surrounding the Credit Bureaus and their purpose are greater than those of any unicorn, monster or boogie man ever created. I must admit to having many misgivings about the purpose of the credit bureau as a young man as well.

As an adolescent of the seventies, I watched my aunts and uncles drive some of the flashiest cars, wear some of the hottest clothes and live in some of the coolest three story flats I'd even seen. Remember that I'm from Saint Louis Missouri. If you know anything about the mid-west, especially Saint Louis, you know that we have our own distinct ideas about cars, coolness and especially fashion. It's rather hard to describe specifically, but, sufficed to say, it would NOT be considered conservative by any stretch of the imagination. Whatever the case, we loved our "over the top" sensibilities. During my impressionable adolescence, I remember seeing my relatives and their friends decked out in chic clothes like full length suede coats with matching vests and pants. They would stroll into my grandmother's house with such swagger; that it looked like they were gliding on air. They always wore the nicest jewelry, the hottest shoes and the most extravagant hats that matched their suits or full length mink coats.

Every Sunday we would have dinner at my grandmother's house and I remember the rows of Lincolns, Cadillacs and luxury cars parked in front of her home. My cousin Lucky and I would often stand on the front porch and choose the car we would drive when we got older. Yes... we played "that's my car" from my grandmother's front porch. We would fantasize about the flashy clothes and cool hats we would wear as we drove down the streets of "the Lou". We even chose the girlfriends who would be riding in the cars with us. My girlfriend was always Pam Grier, of course. As a young teen, I remember conversations at those same Sunday dinners about someone wanting a new luxury item but not being able to get it because of the dreaded Credit Bureau.

I remember hearing adults make statements like, "the credit bureau is messing me up", or "the credit bureau put this or that on my credit so I can't buy"...fill in the blank with whatever extravagance they wanted to purchase. I came to believe that the credit bureau was a huge, dimly lit; smoky building filled with mean people whose sole purpose in life was to make sure they hindered adults from purchasing new things. I grew up thinking that the credit bureau was evil and to be feared. I was also under the impression that there was one credit bureau; after all, adults always said "The" credit bureau. It wasn't until my freshman year of college that I began learning about the true purpose of credit bureaus.

What is a Credit Bureau and what does it do?

The Dictionary of Small Business defines a credit bureau as an agency that collects and sells information about the creditworthiness and ability to meet debt obligations of individuals (consumers) or companies. In the United States, the legal term for a credit bureau, under the federal Fair Credit Reporting Act (FCRA), is a consumer reporting agency, often abbreviated as CRA. Consumer reporting agencies include a wide variety of agencies including credit reporting agencies, mortgage reporting companies, collection services, and tenant screening and employment reporting companies. Credit bureaus provide information to a number of clients. This includes merchants that extend credit to consumers and businesses that, in turn, extend credit to other businesses. Credit bureaus may be private enterprises or may be operated as cooperatives by merchants in a particular geographic area. Users of the services typically pay a fee based on their amount of usage or a flat membership charge.

Credit bureaus neither deny nor grant credit to consumers. Credit can only be granted or denied by the lender where the credit application was filed. Credit bureaus simply serve as clearinghouses for credit history information. Merchants and lenders provide the bureaus with information about how credit customers pay their bills, and the bureaus assemble this information into a file on every consumer or business. Lenders are required to deny or grant credit using a fixed set of criteria; however, your credit report plays a large part in that decision. Credit bureaus are required to record and report accurate information about your credit history; however, it is ultimately up to YOU to verify the accuracy of your credit report.

As previously stated, where there is human interaction there is the possibility of human error. According to Consumer Reports magazine, "48% of consumers have errors in their credit bureau files, many severe enough to result in credit denial"! If you monitor your credit report as you should, most people find at least one error per year on their credit report. It may be something as simple as an incorrect address or zip code or something as major as an incorrect social security number or birth date, which means someone else's information could be listed on your credit history. Whatever the case, you must be diligent in managing your credit report.

Brief history of credit bureaus in America...

As noted in the previous chapter, the basic concept of credit reporting, and early credit bureaus (local merchants who kept records of people who were poor credit risks) can be traced back as early as the 1860's; however, credit reporting agencies experienced rapid growth after World War I. They were originally organized to facilitate the exchange of credit information among merchants. Until the arrival of credit bureaus, the very small amount of credit granted was based on the merchant's personal knowledge of the customer. The earliest credit bureaus only maintained lists of customers who were considered to be poor credit risks. After World War I, the U.S. population became more mobile and credit bureaus expanded to serve a wider audience of merchants. The bureaus filled a void by providing these merchants with information that could be used to make quicker and more accurate decisions on a customer's credit worthiness.

How does the credit bureau fit into the credit process?

The credit report, acquired from the credit bureau, plays a vital part in the credit process from the time that you submit your application for credit. After receiving a completed credit application from you (the consumer) the merchant generally contacts one or more credit bureaus to request your credit report and score. This process is primarily done electronically today. Based on the credit information and score that the merchant receives, the merchant chooses lenders who are more likely to approve your request for credit. The merchant then forwards your application to those lenders. Lenders also have a fixed set of criteria which they use to deny or grant credit. The lenders review the request for credit, the consumer's credit history and score and any other criteria required, and make a decision to deny or grant credit to you. The following chart reflects the consumer credit process from beginning to end:

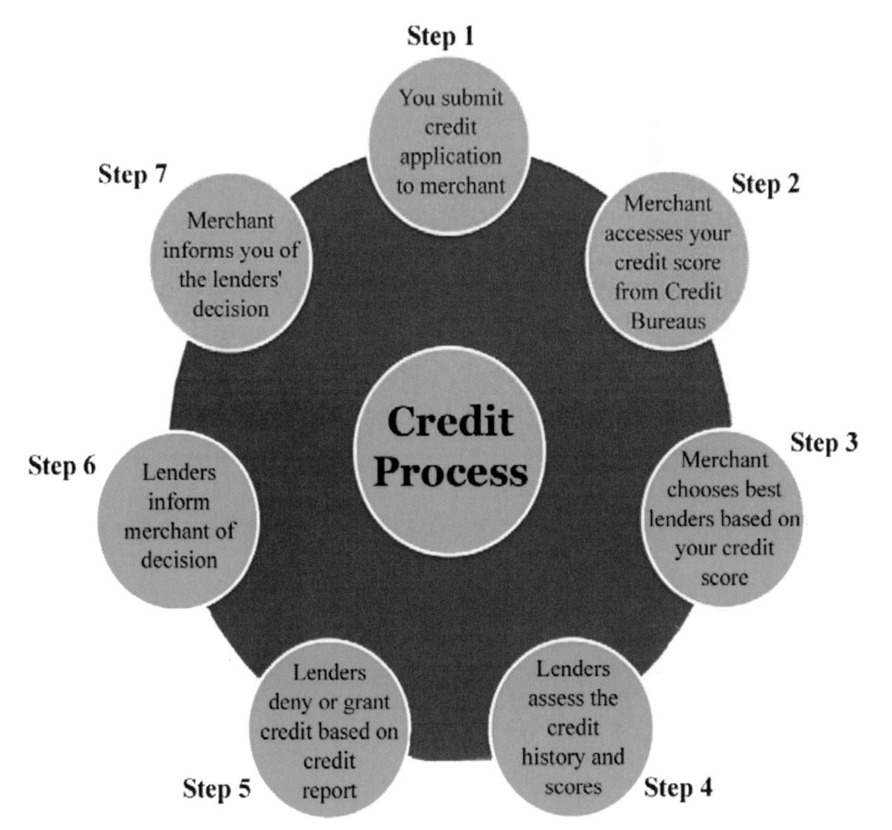

Thanks to high-speed computers and cutting edge electronic data processing, this process can now take place at the speed of light. This quick response allows merchants and lenders to make virtually instantaneous decisions regarding granting or denying credit to consumers.

Are there different types of credit bureaus?
Currently, there are two types of credit bureaus: consumer and commercial. Consumer credit bureaus maintain and report information for individuals, while commercial credit bureaus maintain and report information for businesses. This book focuses, primarily, on consumer credit bureaus; however, information about commercial credit bureaus is included in Session 9 for all of my business owners and future entrepreneurs. Although there are many smaller consumer credit bureaus, the vast majority of lenders today use one or more of the "Big Three" national credit bureaus: Equifax, Experian and TransUnion. We will review the big three, in detail, in the following chapter.

Who regulates credit bureaus?
Credit bureaus house vital information about every consumer with a social security number. That means that every American who has ever applied for credit has a credit file. Many people think that you need to be a certain age before credit bureaus begin tracking your credit history. Unfortunately, that is not the case. Remember the young lady I talked about earlier, whose mother began misusing her credit when she was only 13 years old? It could happen to anyone given the rise in identity theft and credit fraud. With all of your personal information at their disposal, it is important for you to know who regulates the credit bureaus.

The Federal Trade Commission (FTC) and the Office of the Comptroller of the Currency (OCC) regulate, provide oversight and supervise the credit bureaus and companies that furnish data to the credit bureaus. What do these organizations do?

- **The Federal Trade Commission (FTC):**

The Federal Trade Commission has oversight for all consumer credit bureaus.

- **The Office of the Comptroller of the Currency (OCC):**

The Office of the Comptroller of the Currency charters, regulates, and supervises all national banks with regard to the data they furnish credit bureaus.

What governing guidelines do these agencies follow?

The FTC and OCC supervise the credit bureaus using four primary credit bureau regulations and governing guidelines:

- **Fair Credit Reporting Act (FCRA)**

The Fair Credit Reporting Act is a federal law that promotes the accuracy and privacy of information in consumer credit reports. It also controls the use of credit reports and requires consumer reporting agencies to maintain correct and complete files. According to this act, you have a right to review your credit report and to have incorrect information corrected.

- **Fair and Accurate Credit Transactions Act (FACTA)**

The Fair and Accurate Credit Transactions Act of 2003 is a federal law, passed as an amendment to the Fair Credit Reporting Act. This act allows consumers to obtain a free credit report once every twelve months from each of the three major credit bureaus (Equifax, Experian and TransUnion). It also contains provisions to help reduce identity theft and requires secure disposal of consumer information.

❖ **Fair Credit Billing Act (FCBA), and Regulation B**

The Fair Credit Billing Act is a federal law enacted as an amendment to the Truth in Lending Act. Its was enacted to protect consumers from unfair billing practices and to provide a method for addressing billing errors in revolving credit accounts, such as credit card or charge card accounts.

❖ **Equal Credit Opportunity Act (Regulation B)**

Regulation B implements the Equal Credit Opportunity Act. It is a federal law that promotes the availability of credit to all creditworthy applicants without regard to race, color, religion, national origin; sex, marital status or age (provided the applicant has the capacity to contract under state law). The regulation also prohibits the denial of credit merely because an applicant's income may be derived from public assistance sources.

There are far too many details surrounding these laws to review in this book. I would advise you to read the detailed information regarding these four laws and consult an attorney to gain a full understanding of the laws. You should be aware of the bodies that regulate the credit bureaus and the guidelines and standards they are held to. You can contact these agencies directly or visit their websites for further information. Credit bureaus have a number of responsibilities under these regulations and governing guidelines. For all of you knowledge junkies, it would be worth your time to review these regulations, just for fun...and to be fully informed. You will be amazed at your rights, as a consumer.

Homework (Session 8)

It's time to seperate truth from fiction and test your credit bureau knowledge.

Complete the homework for Session 8 in your workbook or e-book.

Consumer Credit Bureaus 102

As complicated as it can sometimes seem, the basic role of credit reporting agencies or credit bureaus is to collect and sell consumer credit information. The consumer credit information is supplied from a wide variety of sources; public records, creditors, lenders, debt collection agencies and other reliable sources with which the credit bureaus have a relationship. The data provided is entered into your personal credit file and maintained, as required by law. The credit bureaus then make your credit file available to your current creditors, prospective lenders and employers as allowed by law. Lenders access the information to assess a consumer's credit worthiness or the ability to meet debt obligations.

There are hundreds of consumer credit bureaus throughout the United States, and most are either owned or under contract with one of the nation's "big three" national consumer credit bureaus: TransUnion, Equifax, and Experian. The three major consumer credit bureaus in the U.S. are affiliated with the Associated Credit Bureaus, Inc. The Associated Credit Bureaus, Inc is an international trade association that represents the consumer credit reporting industry before state and federal legislators. It also represents the industry before the media in consumer credit reporting matters. Over 500 American credit reporting agencies, mortgage reporting companies, collection services, and tenant screening and employment reporting companies are members.

Consumer credit bureaus are growing due, in part, to the approximate one billion credit cards in use in the United States today. A similar number of consumer credit reports are issued annually in the United States. As previously mentioned, two billion pieces of data are entered monthly into credit records. Each of the three major consumer credit bureaus maintain over 190 million credit files, which are used by independent credit reporting agencies across the United States. Many major companies use these credit reports to assess a potential customer's creditworthiness and risk of repayment by using risk-based credit scoring. Risk-based pricing is a rating process based on the different expected risks of different borrowers, as set out in their credit scores. The scores are designed to measure how likely a person is to repay a debt and are a key factor in determining if a person can get credit and at what cost.

The Big Three

As mentioned earlier in the chapter, the vast majority of lenders today use one or more of the "Big Three" credit bureaus: Equifax, Experian and TransUnion. These three credit reporting agencies have emerged as the primary vendors for most consumer credit services. They also have commercial arms within each organization. Each of the three major credit bureaus offers the basic service of collecting, managing and distributing consumer credit information. Although information collected by the big three is supposed to be the same, inconsistencies frequently occur. The three major credit bureaus are all independent of each other and do not share information; in addition, not every merchant uses all three major credit bureaus. Accordingly, the personal financial information that is contained in your credit file at one credit bureau may not be exactly the same as the credit information in another. The individual credit reports will only show information from creditors that participate in that specific credit bureau's services.

There are similarities amongst the big three major credit bureaus; however, the basic function of collecting and selling information for the use of credit reporting is the most prominent. Each of the big three offer different services for consumers. Some of the other similarities include online credit information, ability to dispute information online or via phone, credit notification services and etc. Following is historical information regarding each company.

Equifax

Equifax was founded in 1899 in Atlanta, Georgia as Retail Credit Company. By the 1920's they had offices throughout the US and Canada and by the early 1960's they held information on millions of Americans. Retail Credit Company's willingness to distribute their extensive information to just about anyone, as well as their move to computerize their records led directly to the Federal Fair Credit Reporting Act of 1970. Retail Credit changed its name to Equifax Inc. in 1979. Equifax provides services and systems that serve the financial services of numerous industries, as well as consumer and commercial credit information services, as reported on their website. Visit the Equifax website for additional information regarding their history and services (www.equifax.com).

Experian

Founded in 1980 in Nottingham, England as CCN Systems, Experian moved into the U.S. credit business in 1986 with the acquisition of Management Decisions Systems (MDS). CCN increased their US presence with the 1996 acquisition of TRW Information Systems. Experian.com reports that Experian supports clients in more than 65 countries and has a presence in 38 countries. Experian offers services to consumers that help manage the risk and reward of sound financial decisions, as reported on their website. Experian is a subsidiary of The Great Universal Stores PLC and has headquarters in Nottingham, U.K., and Orange, California. Visit the Experian website for additional information regarding their history and services (www.experian.com).

TransUnion

TransUnion was founded in 1968 in Chicago, Illinois, by Union Tank Car Company as their holding company. TransUnion moved into the credit industry in 1969 and began acquiring smaller regional and major city credit bureaus, which typically had existing contracts with local retailers. In 1969 TransUnion became the first consumer credit reporting agency to replace accounts receivable data with automated tape-to-disc transfer, drastically cutting the time and cost to update consumer files. In the years that followed, TransUnion continued to acquire credit bureaus in other major cities. By 1988, TransUnion established its presence nationally. TransUnion operates nationwide through a network of offices and independent credit bureaus. Visit the TransUnion website for additional information about their history and services (www.transunion.com).

Homework (Session 9)

Think you're ready to run with the big dogs? Let's check your knowledge of the big three.

Complete the homework for Session 9 in your workbook or e-book.

Session 10

Commercial Credit Bureaus 101

Many of my clients are business owners and require information about commercial credit bureaus. Therefore, I've included some information about commercial credit bureaus for my current business owners and my future entrepreneurs.

Commercial credit bureaus sole purpose is to collect maintain and report data for businesses. An accurate and well managed business credit report provides access to important information needed for making knowledgeable business decisions. It can dictate who you do business with, at what price and most importantly who does business with you. Smart business people are aware of their business credit rating and take advantage of the benefits of a good business credit rating. Similarly, recovering from a bad business credit rating is quite difficult.

Just as it is important to maintain a good personal credit rating, it is equally important for your business. Good business credit provides an option for your business even in harsh economic climates. With a good business credit rating, you also have access to cash for expansion, goods, capital expenditures, and access to a wide variety of suppliers. Cash flow and liquidity can be enhanced by business credit as well. Cash solvency allows organizations to take advantage of immediate opportunities without jeopardizing day-to-day operations.

Commercial Credit Reporting Agencies

There are over one hundred commercial credit reporting agencies. Equifax, Experian and TransUnion also have commercial arms and offer many services for commercial clients. One of the major commercial credit reporting agencies in the business is Dun and Bradstreet Corporation. Dun and Bradstreet is a private, for-profit company that reportedly maintains a database on nearly 60 million public and private businesses worldwide. Dun & Bradstreet's websites states that their rating system; "measures a company's business credit rating against other companies in the same field. Data is provided on net worth, equity, number of employees, and financial stability and risk. Other factors include age of the company, trade payments, payment history, and public filings". Most business owners require quick feedback for commercial inquiries, delivered in a concise, ready-to-use format. Commercial credit reporting agencies are increasing their services to meet the needs of large and small businesses in response to that demand.

Should I use a commercial credit agency for my SMALL business?

More commercial credit reporting agencies are beginning to offer information on small businesses. Small businesses are gaining a large share of the overall market. Some of the consumer credit bureaus now offer a commercial credit report that combines a small business owner's personal information with their business information to create a credit risk score. Uncertainty regarding a vendor can put companies at risk if that vendor does not complete their task or supply required product. Commercial credit reports help evaluate those risks. I don't know the specifics about your business; therefore, I cannot advise you, personally, regarding commercial credit services for your business. However, your business plan is one of the best indicators of your need for commercial credit services, specifically your 3 to 5 year growth projections. Choose several commercial credit reporting agencies and review the services offered. If you choose to utilize the services of a commercial credit agency, choose the organization that best fits your current business needs and can be implemented into your plan for growth.

Small business owners must be especially careful regarding their ROI (Return on Investment) because their bottom line is affected more directly than a large corporation's. Therefore, be sure to choose an organization that helps you manage the risks that could affect your bottom line, as well as provide credit information for you and your vendors.

Can commercial credit reports and services enhance my business?

Business owners should always maintain accurate credit information and a good credit status for their business and on their customers. Your business credit reports form the decisions other businesses make about your business, such as:

- What interest rates you will pay for credit
- How much credit is made available to you
- The amount of insurance premiums you will pay
- How much business credit a supplier extends to you
- Investor interest in your business

Remember to request a copy of your business credit report twice a year (minimum) or if you are denied credit. It's up to you to ensure that the information in your business credit report is accurate. This will enable wise, informed financial decisions that allow your business to grow.

Should I monitor the credit status of my customers?

Just as important as monitoring your business credit report, is monitoring the credit status of established customers and potential customers. For most business owners, watching the bottom line is essential to the success of your business. You cannot take risks when offering credit to customers or when applying for credit from vendors. Commercial credit bureaus may offer services to help you mitigate that risk. A commercial credit reporting agency will assist you in monitoring a client or supplier's business credit report. It can offer information such as:

- A supplier's business history
- Client's business status (existing and potential)
- Existing/potential customer's payment history
- Alerts and notifications regarding supplier's or customer's business credit reports
- Information regarding your competitor(s)

How can commercial credit services help my business grow?

Business owners want to offer their customers great service as quickly and efficiently as possible, no matter the size of the organization. Commercial credit bureaus have adapted to the needs of the average business owner by offering commercial reports and services online. The instantaneous access to data and services helps you, the business owner, make informed decisions. A standard web browser will allow you to access all credit information and critical credit data can even be delivered directly to your email address if requested.

Many commercial credit bureaus offer services that allow you to proactively track relationships and monitor issues such as:

- ❖ Monitoring the status of suppliers.
- ❖ Monitoring customers who may be behind on payments.
- ❖ Identifying errors on your credit report that may affect your cash flow position negatively.

Many commercial credit bureaus now incorporate payment history, trade credit history and market demographics on one commercial credit report. This allows you to create important sales, planning and forecasting documentation for your business. Some commercial credit bureaus also offer Human Resources and financial services that help business owners with payroll, tax and employment verification needs.

If you choose to utilize a commercial credit bureau, be sure to review their services and options carefully. If utilized wisely, a commercial credit bureau will not only offer credit check services, it will offer services that help you attract new customers, retain existing customers and assist in the growth of your business.

What information is listed on a Commercial Credit Report?

1. Executive Summary
2. Legal Filings and Collections, trade payment information, trade payment experiences
3. Trade payment totals, additional payment experiences
4. Monthly payment treads, quarterly payment trends, inquiries, government financial profile

5. UCC Profile
6. Commercial Finance relationships, banking relationships – Banking relationships, leasing relationships, insurance bond relationships, company background information.
7. Additional company background information
8. Standard & Poor's Information, Balance sheet, operating statement
9. Critical Data and Ratios

How Can I Increase my Business Credit Rating?

1. Pay your bills on time.

2. Make sure your timely payments are being marked as such in your business profile. This is a part of regular maintenance that you should be performing regularly.

3. Check your business credit at least twice per year, or as changes occur within your company.

4. Consider paying when you receive the product. Your score is based on how fast you pay, not just paying by the due date.

5. Make sure your company has a business listing in your local directory. A business listing shows that you are an established entity, even with a home-based business.

6. Establish "Equity Lines of Credit" for your business BEFORE you need them. Similar to establishing a line of equity for personal use, business lines of credit offer the security of easy access to funds, if required.

7. Keep your personal credit in good standing.

These are a few simple tips that can help you improve and maintain your business credit rating. Proper business credit maintenance should be integrated into your daily business routine. After all, the benefits of a good business credit rating are innumerable!

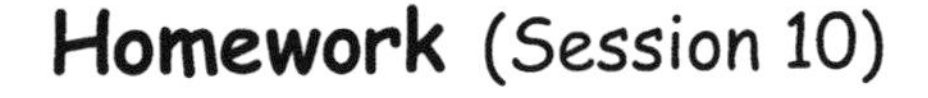

This homework is for all of my current AND future business owners.

Complete the homework for Session 10 in your workbook or e-book.

Session 11

Credit Reports

Do you remember getting report cards in school? For those of us who didn't make excellent grades across the board, it was a true moment of dread. I made excellent grades from first through sixth grade, but something happened when I got to the seventh grade... I discovered girls and there went my excellent grades. From seventh grade through ninth grade, I did very well in some classes, OK in others. However, for some reason, I didn't really think about the cumulative consequences of my "OK" grades until I got my report card and saw the overall affect they had on my GPA. I can still remember how tense that moment was when my teacher handed me my report card in a sealed envelope.

I'd reach out with cold, shaky hands, slowly grasp the envelope and immediately shove it between the pages of my text book. As soon as I put the envelope in the book I would mask my true emotions (horror) by starting a conversation with one of my friends, or joking with a classmate nearby, like it was no big deal. All the while I was freaking out inside wondering what was on that report card. I'd wait until class was over; sneak away to the most isolated, remote part of the school where there was no possibility of anyone finding me. I would open the envelope, ever so slowly, all the while praying that my teachers had remembered that I'd been incredibly nice and helpful to them the previous few days and had somehow found it their hearts to kindly turn my well deserved Ds into Cs. Once I pried the envelope open, I'd peer down at the bright pink piece of paper, lying there in the envelope in all of it's cool pink smugness, just taunting me... yeah smart boy, bet you feel bad about not studying for that English test now don't you, it's time to pay for watching all that TV buddy... go ahead, pull me out, I'm not going to change, I'll just be sitting here in this envelope with the same grades until you decide to pull me out and take a look. After my mind stopped wandering, I'd pull the pink paper out, unfold it and absorb the grades listed as well as the teacher comments, which, for me, generally went something like this: Brian is a smart young man, but he just won't apply himself. Brian is clearly more interested in being the class clown than paying attention in class. And my favorite, Brian asks some very "interesting" questions in class, are you sure he's only 13 years old?

That pink piece of paper simply represented how well I'd managed my school work, homework AND relationships with my teachers for the entire semester. The grades listed on that paper represented what I had earned. There were times when a grade was incorrect and I had to speak with a teacher and have it corrected, but for the most part, I received the grades that I deserved, based on my actions. I learned quickly that I must do the required work and manage my progress. By 9th grade I was wise enough to strive for good grades continually, form a good student/teacher relationship with my teachers, especially the classes that I needed the most help in, and most importantly, I began reviewing my progress reports halfway through each quarter. That way, I always knew what the statuses of my grades were and if there was a problem, I had time to better my grade before the semester grades came out.

That is the same concept of a credit report. Your credit report is the cumulative list of your credit history for the last seven to ten years. In essence, your credit history is summarized on your credit report. As I stated, although there may be errors listed on your credit reports, most of the information listed is true and factual data.... It's what you've earned. Managing your credit report regularly should be a part of your financial management routine. Check your credit at least once per year and have errors corrected immediately! Get your free copy of your credit reports annually, you are entitled to that. If you have had issues and errors in the past, I recommend that you get your credit report twice per year. Remember that the free copy of the credit report does not include credit scores. You will need to request a copy directly from each of the big three credit bureaus individually, unless you order a 3-in-1 credit report. The 3-in-1 report is not included in the free annual credit report, however. Be sure to purchase your credit scores as well, you will need that info.

What is a consumer credit report?

A consumer credit report is "a record of an individual's borrowing and repaying history, compiled and managed by a credit bureau". When you, the consumer, complete an application for credit, your information is forwarded to a credit bureau. The credit bureau matches personal identification information (i.e.: name, address, birth date and etc.) on the applicant for proper identification. The credit bureau then creates a report (credit report) that contains information in the applicant's credit file, which generally spans seven to ten years. The information on the report is used by lenders to ascertain an individual's credit worthiness; or, willingness to repay a debt. The willingness to repay a debt is indicated by past payment history listed on the credit report. Income is another factor in determining whether a lender will grant or deny credit. These factors help lenders determine whether to extend credit, and on what terms. Knowing the status of your credit is one of the most important steps in assessing your current financial situation and understanding your credit report is the first step in that process.

What's listed on a consumer credit report?

Each of the three major credit bureaus offer their own format for credit reports; however, there are five main categories of information in any credit report.

I. **Personal Information**
II. **Account History**
III. **Inquiry Information**
IV. **Public Records**
V. **Other Categories**

Although the exact information and format in these categories may differ, each credit bureau provides this information regarding your personal financial history. Let's examine the various categories of a credit report.

I. Personal Information

The personal information section contains sensitive information that identifies and distinguishes you from any other consumer such as:

a) Your current name and former name (s)
b) Your social security number
c) Your current address and previous addresses
d) Your phone number
e) Your date of birth
f) Your current employer and previous employers

Check your personal information very carefully when reviewing your credit report. One incorrect digit in your birthday or social security number could potentially cause damage to your credit report.

II. Account History Type

This section provides detailed information about all credit accounts in your name. Accounts are divided into five types:

Account History Type		
1	Real Estate	Primary and secondary mortgages
2	Revolving Accounts	Credit cards, open term accounts
3	Installment Accounts	Car loans, fixed term accounts
4	Other	Account where the exact category is unknown
5	Collection Accounts	Accounts assigned to an internal collection department collection agency or attorney.

The following account history information is listed regarding each type of account:

Account History Information		
1	Creditor Name	The name of the lender who gave you the credit.
2	Account Number	The credit account number issued by the lender. Credit bureaus do not issue account numbers.
3	Type	The type or category of the account. *See Account History Type.
4	Condition	Description of the account's payment status as of the last reported date
5	Responsibility	Individual or Joint Account
6	Pay Status	The current state of the account. (i.e.: Open, Closed, Suspended)
7	Date Opened	The date when the account was opened.
8	Date Reported	The last date when any activity in this account was shown. Activities include payments, billings, information updates, etc.)
9	Balance and Limit	The amount you presently owe on the account.
10	Payment and Terms	The amount and number of monthly payments scheduled.
11	High Balance	The most you have ever owed on this account.
12	Past Due	The amount of payment overdue as of the most recent activity.
13	Remarks	Remarks by you or your creditor.
14	2-Yr Payment History	Generally shown as a graphic illustration of your payment history over the past two years.
15	7-Yr Payment History	A record of any late payments that have occurred over the past seven years.

Following is an example of account information that you may find in the Account History section of your credit report:

WILLIS Credit Company

Address:
999 Credit Ave
Anytown, USA 22222
(999) 777-9311

Account Number:
123456789

Status: Past due 90 days

Date Opened:	Type:	Credit Limit/Original Amount:
05/2007	Revolving	$2500
Reported Since:	Terms:	High Balance:
06/2007	12 Months	$5000
Date of Status:	Monthly Payment:	Recent Payment:
04/2010	$150	$150
Last Reported:	Responsibility:	
04/2010	Joint	

Account History:
30 days as of 12-2009
60 days as of 01-2010
90 days as of 02-2010

Two Year Payment History:

CUR	CUR	CUR	CUR	CUR	CUR	CUR	CUR	CUR	CUR	CUR	CUR	CUR	CUR	CUR	CUR	CUR	CUR	CUR	CUR	CUR	30	60	90
Apr	May	Jun	Jul	Aug	Sep	Oct	Nov	Dec	Jan	Feb	Mar	Apr	May	Jun	Jul	Aug	Sep	Oct	Nov	Dec	Jan	Feb	Mar

Seven Year Payment History:

30 Days Late:	1
60 Days Late:	1
90 Days Late:	1

Remarks:

III. Inquiry Information

When a lender requests a copy of your credit report, their name will appear on your credit report, allowing you to monitor who accessed your credit report. There are two types of inquiries; however, the basic rule is to minimize the amount of inquiries on your report as much as possible. Credit inquiries are classified as "hard" or "soft".

Hard Inquiries

Hard inquiries are generated when you complete an application for new credit and the lender requests a copy of your credit report. The number of inquiries over a twelve-month period is tracked and taken into account when your credit score is calculated. An excessive number of hard inquiries have a negative impact on your credit score.

Soft Inquiries

Soft inquiries are generated by your current creditors checking on your status, credit card issuers reviewing your file to see if they wish to extend an unsolicited offer and you personally checking your own credit. Potential lenders don't see soft inquirers when they review your credit report, and they do not impact your credit report. Following is an example of what you may see in the Inquiry Information section of your credit report:

Creditor Name	Date of Inquiry
Willis Credit Company	06/10/2009
ACME Bank	03/22/2009
BPW Credit Card Company	12/01/2008
Real Mortgage Company	09/16/2008
Joe Schmoe Automotive	07/11/2008

IV. Public Records

The public records information section lists publicly available information about legal matters affecting your credit. These records may include judgments against you (civil actions), state or federal tax liens, or bankruptcies. Following is an example of what you may see in the Public Records section of your credit report. The definition for each category is listed as well.

Public Record Information		
1	**Type**	The type of record. (ie: Tax Lien, Bankruptcy, Judgement, etc)
2	**Status**	Current status of the record.
3	**Date Filed/Reported**	Date when the record was initially filed or created.
4	**Filing Method**	Individually or Jointly
5	**Reference Number**	Indentifying number for the record
6	**Closing/Released Date**	Date when the record was closed or the judgement awarded.
7	**Court**	The court or legal agency that has jurisdiction over the record.
8	**Amount**	Dollar amount of the lien or judgement.
9	**Remarks**	Remarks by you or the court.

If the public record is a bankruptcy, three additional fields will be visible:

Public Record Information - Bankruptcy		
1	**Liability**	The amount the court found you to be legally responsible to repay.
2	**Exempt Amount**	A dollar amount claimed against you, but an amount in which the court has decided you are not legally responsible.
3	**Asset Amount**	The dollar amount of total personal assets used in the court's decision.

V. Other Categories

As previously stated, each credit bureau has their own signature format for credit reports. These reports do not vary widely but include some diverse categories amongst each bureau. Following are a few of the other categories that you may find on the various credit reports:

a. Payment History Summary

Credit bureaus may offer summary information. This summary information may offer a single, condensed view of your payment history. It may give you an overall view of your account balances and statuses by the five categories or types listed. The payment history summary section may also summarize your open accounts, closed account, public records and inquiries.

b. Personal Statement

The consumer statement section contains a personal comment that you have submitted to the credit bureau to be added to your report. The personal statement is designed to give you an opportunity to comment on or explain something in your credit history. Please be aware that credit bureaus are required to include the statement, upon their review; however, it has no bearing on your credit score.

c. Creditor Information

The creditor information section lists the names of the creditors that appear in your Account History and Credit Report Inquiry Sections. Each creditor's name, address and phone number is listed. Creditors without listed numbers must be contacted via the U.S. Postal Service.

d. Dispute Information

Most credit bureaus offer information on how disputing erroneous information on your credit report. Disputes can now be submitted online or via mail. Each credit bureau has specific instructions for filing a dispute on their web sites.

Should I obtain a three-in-one credit report?

In today's instant approval world, it is essential for consumers to know where their credit stands. The three major credit bureaus do not share information with each other and the information on each report can be very different. It is important to review all three credit reports and credit scores regularly, as lenders may obtain all 3 credit reports when determining your ability to repay a loan. Each credit bureau offers a 3-in1 credit report to consumers. This particular report shows information and scores for all three credit bureaus on one report. The three-in-one credit report is not covered by the FTC law guaranteeing a free credit report once per year. The guaranteed free report only applies to singular credit reports from the individual credit bureaus.

The three major credit bureaus offer three-in-one credit reports as a service. The fees for each service vary and the score may be an additional cost. If you are interesting in obtaining a three-in-one credit report and score, please go directly to the credit bureau's individual websites to obtain detailed information.

The four main categories of information offered on the three-in-one report is still the same; however, instead of viewing information from an individual credit bureau, the same information for all three credit bureaus is listed on one report. Similar to the individual credit reports, each of the big three offers their own format for 3-in-1credit reports. Following is an example of what you may see in the Personal Information section of a 3-in-1 credit report.

Three-in-One Credit Report

Personal Information

	Experian	TransUnion	Equifax
Name:	Joseph Schmoe	Joseph Schmoe	Joseph Schmoe
Current Address:	800 Good Credit Rd	800 Good Credit Rd.	801 Good Credit Ln
Previous Address:	Anytown USA 11111	Anytown USA 11112	Anytown USA 11111
Current Employer:	BPW Credit Company	BPW Credit Company	ABC Credit Company

The account history information is similarly listed with the type and history categories as noted in section two of this chapter. Following is an example of what you may see in the Account History section of a 3-in-1 credit report.

Creditor: WILLIS Credit Company

	Experian	TransUnion	Equifax
Account Number:	2468123	1232468	2468123
Type:	Revolving	Revolving	Real Estate
Condition:	Open	Open	Open
Responsibility:	Joint	Individual	Individual
Date Opened:	05/2007	05/2007	05/2007
Date Reported:	04/2010	05/2010	04/2010
Balance and Limit:	$2000	$2500	$2500
Pay Status:	90 days late	60 days late	90 days late
Payment & Terms:	$260/24mths	$260/24 mths	$260/24 mths
High Balance:	$5000	$5000	$5000
Past Due:	$780	$520	$780
Remarks:			

Two Year Payment History:

	Apr	May	Jun	Jul	Aug	Sep	Oct	Nov	Dec	Jan	Feb	Mar
Experian:	CUR	CUR	CUR	CUR	CUR	CUR	CUR	CUR	CUR	CUR	CUR	CUR
TransUnion:	CUR	CUR	CUR	CUR	CUR	CUR	CUR	CUR	CUR	CUR	CUR	CUR
Equifax:	CUR	CUR	CUR	CUR	CUR	CUR	CUR	CUR	CUR	CUR	CUR	CUR

	Apr	May	Jun	Jul	Aug	Sep	Oct	Nov	Dec	Jan	Feb	Mar
Experian:	CUR	CUR	CUR	CUR	CUR	CUR	CUR	CUR	CUR	30	60	90
TransUnion:	CUR	CUR	CUR	CUR	CUR	CUR	CUR	CUR	CUR	CUR	30	60
Equifax:	CUR	CUR	CUR	CUR	CUR	CUR	CUR	CUR	CUR	30	60	90

Seven Year Payment History:

	Experian	TransUnion	Equifax
30 Days Late:	1	1	1
60 Days Late:	1	1	1
90 Days Late:	1	0	1

Following is an example of what you may see in the Inquiry Information section of a 3-in-1 credit report:

Inquiry Information

Creditor Name	Date of Inquiry	Credit Bureau
BPW Credit Company	03/01/2010	Equifax
Joe Schmoe Real Estate	11/12/2009	TransUnion
I.O.U. Bank	09/22/2009	Experian
LVW Mortgage Company	06/28/2009	TransUnion
Little J Department Store	02/10/2009	Equifax

The public records information is similarly listed with the type and categories as noted in section four of this chapter. Following is an example of what you may see in the Public Records section of a 3-in-1 credit report:

BANKRUPTCY

	Experian	TransUnion	Equifax
Type:	Chapter 13	Chapter 13	Chapter 13
Status:	Filed	Filed	Filed
Date Filed:	06/2004	06/2004	06/2004
How Filed:	Joint Account	Joint Account	Joint Account
Reference #:	86-75-309	86-75-309	86-75-309
Closing Date:	05/15/2006	05/15/2006	05/15/2006
Court:	County Court	County Court	County Court
Liability:	$12, 500	$12,500	$12,500
Exempt Amount:	$2,500	$2,500	$2,500
Asset Amount:	$4,000	$4,000	$4,000

Who Is Allowed to See Your Credit Report?

Credit bureaus can provide information to the following requestors:

1) Prospective or existing creditors.

2) Employers considering you for employment, promotion, reassignment, or retention.

3) Insurers considering you for an insurance policy or reviewing an existing policy.

4) Government agencies reviewing your government benefits or financial status.

5) Persons or organizations with a legitimate business need for the information.

Credit bureaus may also furnish reports by court order or federal jury subpoena. In addition, they will issue your credit report to a third party if you request it in writing.

Just FYI...
Credit bureaus are required, by law, to help you understand your report. If you have any questions regarding your credit report, each of the major credit bureaus have information on their website regarding their specific credit report format. They are also obligated to answer any questions you have regarding your credit report format or information directly. This is a free service required by law; therefore, you should never be charged a fee for this information.

Homework (Session 11)

What does your credit report say about you... and how you change that?

Complete the homework for Session 11 in your workbook or e-book.

Credit (Risk) Scores

Your credit report is a detailed, seven to ten year history of your credit transactions. Your credit score, on the other hand, is a three digit numerical expression of your credit file based on a statistical analysis. Put quite simply, your credit score offers creditors an overall view of your current credit status using a three digit number. This three digit scoring system was designed to inform potential lenders of your rating as a credit risk using a specific numerical model. Now that we are quite educated about credit bureaus and credit reports, let's educate ourselves about credit scoring and modeling.

FACTA defines a "credit score" as: "A numerical value or a categorization derived from a statistical tool or modeling system used by a person who makes or arranges a loan to predict the likelihood of certain credit behaviors, including default. The numerical value derived from such analysis may also be referred to as a 'risk predictor' or risk score". The basic premise of a credit risk score is rather simple; the higher the score, the less risk you pose to creditors, the lower the score the more risk you pose and the more time it will take to manage your account. Your credit score is based on credit report information and represents the "perceived" likelihood of your paying debts on time. Your credit score is based on information in your credit report in its current state, and on all credit related data, not just negative data.

Information on your credit report is typically compiled from credit bureaus or credit reporting agencies. Lenders use credit scores to evaluate potential risk and to determine who qualifies for a loan, at what interest rate, and what credit limits. In addition to lenders, other organizations, such as mobile phone companies, insurance companies, government departments and now many employers require credit checks. Your credit score isn't the only determining factor of whether you are granted or denied credit and at what interest rate, but it is a very important factor. Credit scores differ depending on the credit bureau, which credit scoring agency is used and which credit scoring model is used. Lenders may request specific information based on the type of credit being applied for, therefore, a credit score may also vary depending on the score model requested (i.e.: Auto, Mortgage, etc).

As you read further, please remember that credit scores provide odds, not certainties. Credit scoring models cannot pinpoint a consumer's credit history without error because there are often variables that cannot be included in the model. That is why it is vital for you to manage your credit report to ensure accuracy at all times. You want the advantage of having accurate information in your credit history file so that these models are run with accurate information.

Why does my credit score matter?

Individuals with higher credit scores are offered different services as those with lower scores. Individuals with lower credit scores are generally targeted with subprime loans with higher interest rates and Annual Percentage Rates (APR). You have probably heard a lot about subprime loans related to mortgages; however, subprime lending can apply to any industry offering loans. If an individual has a subprime loan on their credit report, it can damage their credit score. The lower score, in turn, attracts more subprime loans, resulting in a vicious cycle. Furthermore, sub-prime and predatory loans are disproportionately made to minorities. The Equal Credit Opportunity Act forbids creditors from considering race, sex, marital status, national origin, and religion when reviewing a credit application.

Your credit score can be affected by late payments, non payments, length of credit history and the size of account balances in relation to your credit limits. Remember that the credit score is not the sole factor that decides whether you are denied or granted credit; however it is one of the major factors.

What is a credit scoring agency and credit scoring model?

A credit scoring agency is a company that collects your credit history from a credit bureau and offers a credit scoring model (or system) that takes your credit report history and calculates it using five main categories:

- Payment history
- Outstanding balances
- Credit history
- Type of credit
- New credit

These categories have varying levels of importance. Credit scoring models offer a three digit credit score that represents the likelihood of your repaying the credit on time and as promised. Credit scoring agencies offer their versions of credit scoring models to the credit bureaus; however, credit bureaus are not legally obligated to use any particular credit scoring model. Various industries, such as mortgage lenders, credit card companies, automobile lenders and etc. generally use the same credit reporting model, in order to keep a level of consistency throughout the industry. In fact, some larger lenders have developed their own, proprietary scoring models which they use exclusively. Credit bureaus generally follow industry best practices where credit scoring agencies and models are concerned. Historically, the big three credit bureaus have tended to utilize the same "primary" credit scoring agency and model in order to offer a certain amount of consistency in the credit scoring process. Although there are numerous credit scoring agencies, we will focus on the two major players within the consumer credit scoring industry; Fair Isaac Company and their FICO® credit scoring model and the VantageScore credit scoring model.

Tell me about Fair Isaac Company...

Disclaimer: Although the algorithm for calculating a FICO® Score is not 100% transparent, Fair Isaac offers general guidelines that let individuals get a feel for why their score is where it is.

The oldest and most widely used credit scoring agency in the United States is the Fair Isaac Company. Fair Isaac Company's website notes that they are the leading provider of credit scoring, decision management, fraud detection and credit risk score services.

A bit of Fair Isaac Company history...

Fair Isaac Company was founded in 1956 when an engineer, Bill Fair, and mathematician, Earl Isaac, designed the first credit risk scoring model. Fair Isaac Company introduced its first versions of the credit scoring model to department stores, banks and hotels from the early 1960s through the 1970s and introduced the first version of the risk scoring model, designed specifically for credit bureaus, in 1981. The three major credit bureaus purchase the credit risk scoring product from Fair Isaacs Company then license and distribute the product under their company's title. The first version of the general-purpose FICO® risk scoring model was debuted by Equifax in 1989.

Equifax named the product BEACON and thusly began offering the BEACON credit risk score model to their vendors. Their vendors, which are banks, lenders, mortgage companies and etc, utilized the credit risk score model to determine credit worthiness for you, the consumer. TransUnion implemented the FICO® model in 1991 and dubbed it EMPIRICA. Experian followed suit in 1991 as well, dubbing their version Fair Isaac or Fair Isaac II. One of Fair Isaac's big boon came in 1995 when Fannie Mae and Freddie Mac recommended the use of FICO® scores for evaluating all national mortgage loans. The Fair Isaac Company revised its FICO® scoring model again in 2000 naming the updated version FICO® NextGen. The big three credit bureaus made FICO® NextGen available to vendors in 2001 with Equifax naming their version Pinnacle, TransUnion's version being named PRECISION and Experian dubbing their version Fair Isaac Advanced Risk Score.

The Fair Isaac Company revised its FICO® credit risk scoring model numerous times since 1989. Their latest version, FICO 08, was released in 2008. The specific version names and roll-out dates by the individual credit bureaus are not available as of this writing. The new FICO 08 credit risk scoring model is reportedly more forgiving of occasional slips by consumers, but will take a harder line on repeat offenders.

How do the FICO scoring models calculate my credit score?

The FICO NextGen scoring model is still the primary scoring model being used by many vendors to calculate credit scores; however, the latest version, FICO 08 is ready to be implemented, as of this writing (2009). Since both versions are currently available, let's review FICO® NextGen and FICO 08 scoring models to find out how the models calculate your credit score.

FICO NextGen... *(Current model)*

The FICO NextGen credit risk scoring model was developed by analyzing statistics and picking out various characteristics that are believed to relate to creditworthiness. FICO NextGen credit scores are calculated from the credit information in your credit report grouped into the following categories: Payment History, Outstanding Balance(s), Credit History, Types of Credit, New Credit Cards. Although the scoring model is basically the same for each credit bureau, the actual score is based on the credit data available in your credit file. Not all lenders choose to report to each of the big three credit bureaus, therefore, your credit score may vary from bureau to bureau. As previously noted, a credit score may also vary, depending on the credit scoring model requested (i.e.: automobile, mortgage etc).

The following pie chart shows the percentages used in the five categories calculated to create your credit score.

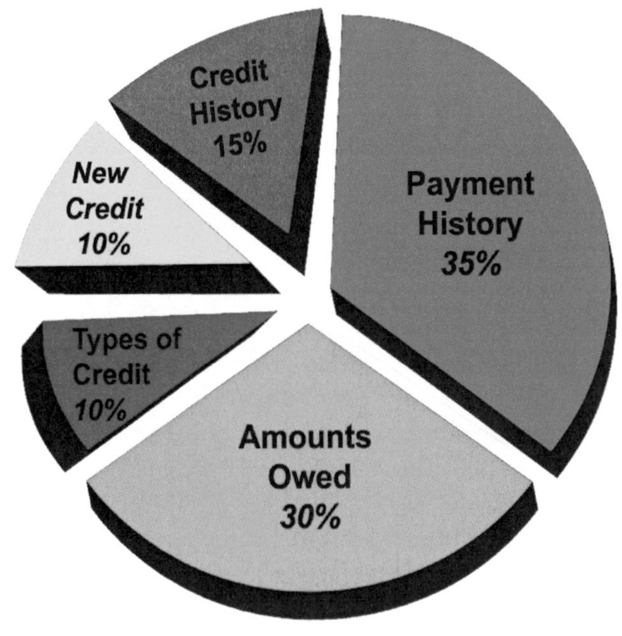

35% Payment History
30% Amounts Owed
15% Credit History
10% Type of Credit
10% New Credit

The percentages in the pie chart reflect the importance of each category in determining your FICO NextGen credit score. Following is additional detail regarding each category.

Payment History (35%)
The Payment History category takes into account your payment history for the last seven to ten years. Accounts that have been paid on time are shown in "current" status. Negative payment history consists of late payments, bankruptcies, collections, charge-offs and judgments. This category is used to measure your ability to pay your bills on time.

Amounts Owed (30%)
The Amounts Owed category takes into account your total amount of credit outstanding versus the maximum amount creditors are willing to extend to you.

Credit History (15%)
The Credit History category takes into account the length of time accounts have been opened. This category shows how long you have had credit established and takes into account how well you've managed those accounts since establishing them.

Type of Credit (10%)
This category takes into account the types of credit you have established: banks versus finance companies, revolving credit versus installment accounts, real estate accounts or other. Certain types of accounts are looked upon more favorably than others.

New Credit (10%)
This category takes into account the number of times you have applied for credit in the recent past. It also takes into account the amount of and credit inquiries in the recent past as well. New credit obviously changes your debt to income ratio and inquiries show that you are actively looking to open new credit accounts, which could affect your debt to income ratio as well.

Although I do not have the exact formula for the FICO NextGen credit risk model, these are the primary categories and percentage for calculating your FICO NextGen credit score.

What is the FICO NextGen credit score range?
The FICO NextGen score range for the three major credit reporting agencies is 300 – 850, with 300 being the lowest possible score and 850 being the highest. Individuals with

higher credit scores are offered different services than those with lower scores. When lenders request scores from the three credit bureaus, they generally use the "middle score" as an average of the three scores. Since the big three credit bureaus scores vary so widely, lenders generally discard the highest and lowest credit scores and base their decisions on the middle score. Example: These are your credit scores from the big three credit bureaus:

Equifax: 620
TransUnion: 740
Experian: 680

In this scenario, the lender would more-than-likely use 680 as the credit score to decide your credit worthiness, thereby, using your "middle" score. A credit score of 720 or higher will allow you to receive good interest rates and services. A credit score of 750 or higher will allow you to receive the best offers for interest rates and services. Interest rates vary depending on the fluctuation of the market.

FICO 08... *(Latest Revision)*
Just as I began to feel comfortable with the FICO NextGen credit risk scoring model, the Fair Isaac Company releases a new version, FICO 08. FICO 08 is similar to the FICO NextGen scoring model in most respects. The new scoring model will retain the same numerical range (300 - 850), minimum scoring criteria, and risk scoring categories as the FICO NextGen model

- **Payment History**
- **Outstanding Balances**
- **Credit History**
- **Types of Credit**
- **New Credit Cards**

The percentage of each risk scoring category has yet to be made public. Fair Isaac Company reports that "the primary reason for the planned switch to FICO 08 has to do with the forecasting powers of the new model". Due to the leniency of loans during the sub-prime boom, Fair Isaac saw a need to update the model to better predict loan default. Fair Isaac reports that FICO 08 will do a better job at predicting the likelihood of default on a loan by making several changes to its existing model.

What are some highlights of the new FICO 08 scoring model?

✓ **Delinquencies**

A big change in the scoring model has to do with payment patterns, especially those that are greater than 90 days late in making a payment. The FICO 08 model will be more forgiving to consumers that are in arrears in one area, but have a number of other accounts that are in good standing.

> ***Example 1:*** The new formula ignores small collection accounts, charge-offs and repossessions in which the original debt was less than $100. This is a big victory for consumers because minor debts (i.e.: unpaid library fines, forgotten parking tickets or a small medical bill) had a major impact on credit scores.

> ***Example 2:*** The new version is reportedly less punishing to those who have had a serious credit setback, such as a charge-off or repossession, as long as their other active credit accounts are all in good standing.

✓ **Piggybacking**

FICO 08 won't take into consideration credit-card accounts for authorized users. Piggybacking allows individuals with bad or no credit to leverage the payment history of the primary card holder by adding the individual's name to an existing credit card account as an authorized user. This generally helps the individual with bad or no credit by creating a longer (and hopefully) more positive credit history.

✓ **Property Value**

Property value forecasts, another big factor in the subprime collapse, are also outside the score's scope in the new model.

✓ **Available Credit**

It is even more sensitive than the classic FICO as to how much of your available credit you're using. The new scoring system penalizes to a greater degree borrowers who use a high percentage of their available credit. (Warning: If your credit card issuer slashes your credit limit, which is increasingly likely these days, you could see your scores plunge, regardless of whether you carry a balance)

✓ **Active Credit**

The new scoring formula also responds more negatively if consumers have few open, active accounts. So make sure to use your oldest cards at least quarterly in order to keep them active. This will raise increase the number of accounts in good standing.

✓ **Serious Delinquency**

FICO 08 will draw greater distinctions among borrowers who are at least 90 days late in making a loan payment, known as a serious delinquency. Traditionally, many credit-scoring models grouped subprime consumers into one general category. But Fair Isaac says its new model will give a higher score to a borrower in arrears if they also have a number of other credit accounts in good standing. Conversely, a person's score could drop if he or she has multiple delinquent accounts.

- ✓ **Credit Types**

FICO 08 gives more points to consumers who maintain a variety of credit types, such as credit accounts, mortgage and auto loan; because it shows they can manage payments on different types of loans.

Will the new FICO 08 scoring model affect my credit score right away?

The answer varies for each individual. Keep in mind that credit scores are used by many lenders to determine the amount of credit to extend a borrower, therefore, the model used to determine that credit score is quite important to know. Here are some examples of how the new FICO 08 credit scoring model might affect your credit score:

- ✓ If you have at least one major account in delinquency, but you also have a number of accounts in good standing with creditors, then your credit score would likely increase / improve with the new FICO 08 credit scoring model. Why... because although you have a delinquency, most of your other accounts are current and in good standing.

- ✓ If you have at least one major account in delinquency, and you demonstrate a poor payment pattern with several other accounts with creditors, then your credit score would likely decrease / deteriorate with the new FICO 08 credit scoring model. Why... because you have numerous delinquent accounts, which shows a common pattern.

- ✓ If you have three credit accounts open and one is with a mortgage account, one is a credit card and one is an auto loan, then your credit score would likely increase / improve with the new FICO 08 credit scoring model. Why... because you have a variety of credit types.

- ✓ If you have three varying credit accounts open and they are all credit card accounts, then your credit score would likely decrease/deteriorate with the new FICO 08 credit scoring model. Why... because you need a variety of credit types with the new model.

Examples provided by Fair Isaac indicate that some consumers might experience a 20 to 25 point adjustment to their credit scores, given specific conditions. However, the most effective way to improve your credit score is by ensuring the information used to generate the score is accurate. No matter what scoring model is being used, make sure the information in your credit file is accurate; this is the information that Fair Isaac relies on to come up with its score. Be sure to secure a copy of your credit report and scores from each of the big three credit bureaus to ensure that there are no errors or missing information.

Tell me about the VantageScore credit scoring model...

The big three credit bureaus: Equifax, Experian and TransUnion, came together and developed VantageScore Solutions LLC. VantageScore Solutions LLC then developed their own proprietary credit scoring model, dubbed VantageScore. The VantageScore credit scoring model was formed in 2006 and is fully owned by the three major credit bureaus. VantageScore.com reports that a team of top statisticians, analysts and credit data experts from each of the big three credit reporting agencies built the underlying algorithms or VantageScore, "to offer the marketplace a highly predictive and consistent scoring approach to determine consumer creditworthiness". It has also been reported that the model was created in response to the relaxed credit standards that helped the subprime fiasco to flourish.

The VantageScore scoring model is offered by the big three credit bureaus but is not widely used in the U.S. as of this writing (Q1 2009). We do not have a large amount of history or usage data to research and cite as of this writing, neither can we substantiate or dispel VantageScore's claim that the new system is superior to any existing system. We can, and will report the scoring model features, as reported by VantageScore Solutions, LLC.

How does the VantageScore scoring model calculate my credit score?

Although the VantageScore scoring model is new and reported as a more intuitive form of credit scoring, it has a large number of similarities to the FICO credit scoring model. VantageScore credit scores are primarily calculated from the credit data in your credit report grouped into the following categories:

- **Payment History**
- **Credit Utilization**
- **Credit Balances**
- **Depth of Credit**
- **Recent Credit**
- **Available Credit**

Similar to the FICO scoring model, each of the three credit bureaus offer the same VantageScore algorithm to provide credit scores; however, the actual score is based on the credit data available in your credit file. Not all lenders choose to report to each of the big three credit bureaus, therefore, your credit score may vary from bureau to bureau. As previously noted, a credit score may also vary, depending on the score model requested (Automobile, Mortgage etc).

The following pie chart shows the percentages used in the six categories calculated to create your VantageScore credit score.

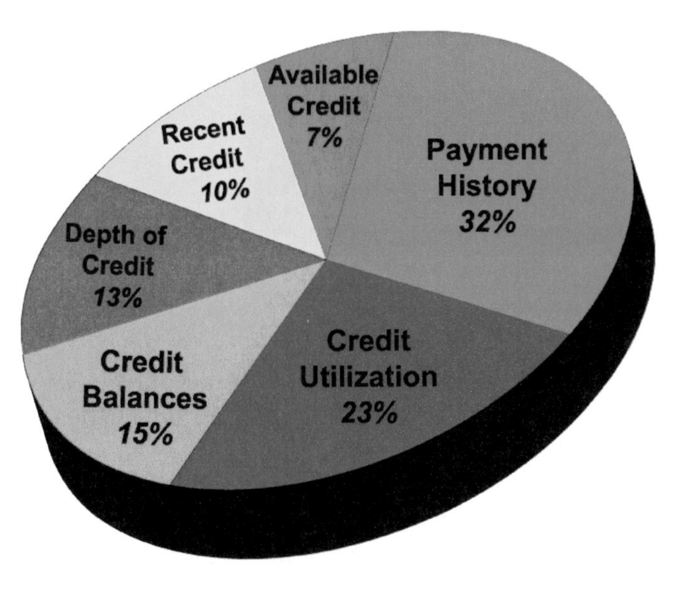

32% Payment History
23% Credit Utilization
15% Credit Balances
13% Depth of Credit
10% Recent Credit
7% Available Credit

The percentages in the chart reflect the importance of each category in determining your VantageScore credit score. Following is additional detail regarding each category.

Payment History (32%)
The Payment History category takes how timely and consistent your payments are.

Credit Utilization (23%)
The Credit Utilization category takes into account your debt-to-credit ratios and how much credit is available.

Credit Balances (15%)
The Credit Balances category takes your total debt into account. Most likely, delinquent debt is counted more harshly than current debt.

Depth of Credit (13%)
The Depth of Credit category takes into account the length of credit history.

Recent Credit (10%)
The Recent Credit category takes into account how recent and many new hard inquiries and new accounts there are.

Available Credit (7%)
The Available Credit category takes into account how much credit can be accessed, for example, could you spend $50,000 of credit tonight or within the next week.

What is the VantageScore credit score range?
The VantageScore credit score range is probably the biggest difference between the VantageScore and FICO models. As previously stated, the FICO score range for the three major credit bureaus is 300 – 850, with 300 being the lowest possible score and 850 being the highest. The

VantageScore credit scores range for the three major credit bureaus is 501 – 990, with 501 being the lowest possible score and 990 being the highest. The VantageScore score range consists of both a number and letter grade and reportedly uses a simple single formula to evaluate your credit risk profile.

A = 901–990 (Super prime)
B = 801–900 (Prime plus)
C = 701–800 (Prime)
D = 601–700 (Nonprime)
F = 501–600 (High risk)

As you can see, VantageScore capitalizes on the familiar academic scale which makes it rather simple to associate your score to a letter grade. Following are the definitions for each of the grade scores, as reported by VantageScore.com:

A (901 - 990) Super Prime
Consumers in this group are scoring in the top 11% of the population. Consumers in this category are likely to be viewed as a very low credit risk by most lenders. Lenders are likely to offer their best rates and terms to consumers in this score range.

B (801 - 900) Prime Plus
Consumers in this category have exhibited good credit management. Consumers in this category are scoring in the top 40% of the population. Most lenders offer their "good" rates to consumers in this category, and some will offer better terms.

C (701 - 800) Prime
Consumers in this category are scoring in the top 60% of the population. Lenders typically view this category as

creditworthy and may offer reasonable terms to consumers within this score range. Some lenders may wish to review the credit history of consumers in this category in more depth and may require additional documentation in order to extend favorable terms.

D (601 - 700) Non-Prime
Consumers in this category are scoring in the lowest 38% of the population. Lenders typically view consumers in this category as higher risk. While many lenders still make credit available, they will likely offer somewhat less favorable terms to compensate for higher default rates in this category.

F (501 - 600) High Risk
This category represents the lowest-scoring 19% of the population. Lenders generally view this as a very risky group. Many prefer not to extend credit to this group. Others may extend credit but require deposit accounts to protect the loan. Some will extend more traditional credit but require much higher interest payments to compensate for the increased risk associated with this category.

VantageScore does not use the "middle score" process, as the letter/number scoring process allows for designation of credit status without the sliding scale.

What can I expect from the VantageScore scoring model?

- ✓ **Thin Credit History**

VantageScore reportedly provides higher credit ratings to people with "thin" credit history files, such as:

a. young adults just starting their careers
b. recently divorced or widowed individuals with little or no credit in their own name

c. newly arrived immigrants
d. previous bankrupts
e. people who shun the traditional banking system by choice

✓ **Singular Model**

With VantageScore each of the three credit bureaus use singular scoring model; however, results will vary depending on the data reported at each credit bureau.

✓ **New Product**

VantageScore's biggest claim to fame is the scoring model, which is reportedly easier to understand and more consistent than other scoring models. VantageScore is a new product and has not been industry tested; therefore, I do not have as much information to supply.

Please be advised that I am not advocating any particular credit scoring models; I am simply giving you the facts. There's nothing wrong with good old fashioned competition; in fact, it may work well in our favor. How you ask? Both Fair Isaac Company and VantageScore Solutions LLC are in business to be successful and most business people know that competition is one of the best ways of bringing prices down and forcing companies to improve their product. Most importantly, the big three credit bureaus promise to provide clear guidelines about what goes into the scores and how consumers can better their numbers. It is yet to be seen just how specific those guidelines are. Either way, the ongoing dialogue around making the scoring models more transparent to us, the consumers, is always a good thing.

How will I know which model is being used when I apply for credit?

The short answer is, you won't unless you ask. Even if you

ask, you may not be given the information. Remember that the credit model has changed along with our economy. Lenders aren't as eager to lend credit as they were some two or three years ago and credit scoring models have been updated to reflect that. It would still benefit you to ask the potential lender which credit scoring model they use before you even apply for credit. If they give you the information, you can then check your credit in advance of applying for credit from the lender. Knowing your credit score and the credit model used will help you choose which lender to go to, the type of interest rate and APR that should be offered to you, the most likely outcome of your credit application and what type of bargaining leverage you have. Remember, credit scoring models are tools used by lenders to help decide your credit worthiness. It is still up to you to proactively manage your credit to ensure that their model has accurate data to work with.

One of my clients once said to me, "Brian, I appreciate you helping me with my credit, but I still don't see how credit scores really help us... the "regular" people? I had to think about that one for a moment before responding. As a consumer, and someone who has done rather extensive research about credit scores, I responded that from everything I've read and researched credit scores were not designed primarily to help "regular" people, better known as... the consumer. Credit risk scoring models are packaged product designed for and sold to credit bureaus and credit reporting agencies. Credit bureaus and credit reporting agencies purchase and rename the product and in turn offer it to their vendors for consumer and commercial credit assessment. Like many consumer driven product, the need from commercial vendors drive the product to consumers. That's just the way it is.

Like many other things in our lives, you must consider credit maintenance and education something that we have to do in order to "play the game"... and in the words of Nike, "Just do it"! I hope that someone comes along and changes the system so that it favors the consumer more than the vendors. But until you do, your best defense is education, awareness and action. Always know the rules, and the model, so you can play the game well!

Homework (Session 12)

Let's work on getting those numbers as high as possible!

Complete the homework for Session 11 in your workbook or e-book.

Building Credit

<u>An Open Letter to High School & College Students</u>

Students,

Let me be the first adult to apologize to you in advance! I am truly sorry for the horrible economic mess that we are dropping in your collective lap. Our greed, selfishness and arrogance allowed us to recklessly mismanage your generation's finances; however, you will have the responsibility of fixing it. We squandered our good name and credit internationally and leave you with the ragged remains of our country's reputation, in hopes that you will somehow mend it and make it better for your children. We have no excuse for what we did, though some of us constantly attempt to find one.

Those of us who have your best interests at heart know that you are our hope for a better tomorrow. In order for you to start off on the right foot, we want to prepare you for the mess that we've left. We pray that you find the fortitude, strength and courage to be the people that we could have been: responsible with your time, mindful of your talent and firm in your truth. Although we shamefully lay this battered and bloodied economy at your young feet, we do offer our abiding love and sincere prayers that you win the battle of flesh. We...did not.

Sincerely,

Brian

This credit process probably seems overwhelming to you right now. I'm an adult but I still remember that the responsibilities of the teen and young adult years can be quite overwhelming. Credit, finances and anything else dealing with financial responsibility was the last thing on my mind when I was a high school student, and even in my first year of college. I was well on my way to graduating from college before I really got serious about actively managing my credit and finance. That was a HUGE mistake for me but I want to help you avoid that mistake while you are young. I'm a very successful 45 year old man; however, if I had learned about credit and finance management while in high school, I could have been successful by 25 or 30 years old. I don't make that statement with regret, I make it in the hopes that you will learn from my mistakes. I want to help you prepare yourself for life as early as possible because life is coming whether you're ready for it or not. I not only want to help you be prepared for life, I want to set you up for success in life! So... let's dig in.

You may not be aware of it but... the availability of credit, as we knew it, has changed. That statement is not meant to frighten you, it is meant to make you aware so that you can be prepared. Your parents and I grew up in a world where we could buy almost anything we wanted, whenever we wanted because we had access to more credit than we ever needed. It sometimes didn't even matter whether our credit was good or bad, most of us could purchase things completely out of our price range whenever we wanted to because there was always someone willing to extend credit to us. If we had good credit, we would get whatever we wanted for a lower interest rate and if we had bad credit we could generally get most things we wanted even though we paid a much higher interest rate and monthly payments. We lived in a fantasy world for a long long time. I call it a fantasy world because it was a world where we could get luxury items and other "wants" whether we'd been responsible with our credit or not. We should have known that a world like that couldn't exist forever. Sufficed to say, the excessive credit-fueled fantasy world is now gone! This little thing called the credit crisis of 2007 changed all of that for us and you.

Some people blame the overall credit crisis solely on the sub-prime mortgage bust, stating that too many people bought houses that they could not afford, which created the credit crisis. I beg to differ. The sub-prime bust played the most obvious part in the crisis; however, it was not the sole reason. Earlier in the book I stated that this crisis has been over 20 years in the making. When it became easy for almost EVERYONE to gain access to unlimited amounts of credit, and people began owing five times their salaries for extravagance... the credit crisis began. I personally trace it back to the early eighties, my era. It was the era of BMWs, Yuppies, Buppies, lavish condos uptown, extravagant travel and luxury as far as the eye could see. We were dubbed the "me" generation and we lived up to that name whole heartedly. The stock market was king and everybody rode the wave of prosperity. The problem came about when we stopped using common sense with our credit and finances. We did not follow our own advice and live by the simple lessons that our parents tried to teach us. Simple rules like:

- What goes up must come down.
  (i.e.: the stock market, economy)

- Save your money and one day it may save you.

- If something looks too good to be true it probably is. *(i.e.: A pre-approved ten thousand dollar credit card for a high school or college student with no job)*

- You can't get something for nothing.
  (i.e.: buying a $500 thousand dollar home on a $25 thousand dollars a year salary)

- Too much of a good thing is not good for you.
  (i.e.: excess credit = excess debt)

And of course, my grandmother's sage advice:

- If you can't buy it with cash, you probably don't need it!

These are some of the basic tenants of life, let alone credit. Hopefully, you will do as we say, not as we did when it comes to responsibility with your credit and finances. This chapter is designed to help you start off on the right foot and the rest of the book is designed to help you stay there. This is a road map from high school to college showing you how to best establish, manage and protect your credit.

High School Students

If you are a new high school student, you are probably trying to get a handle on high school expectations and where you fit in at school. If you are a seasoned high school student, your GPA and college applications are most likely at the forefront of your thinking. And if you are a college student, you are probably trying to make it through school and get ready for the real world at the same time. I completely understand how you all feel. I hope that you are, at minimum, a freshman in high school reading this book and preparing yourself for college. Realistically, I will assume that you are a junior or senior in high school (at minimum) or a college student. Either way, this chapter includes a plan and tips specifically for you to help you start out on the right path, and stay there. Be sure to follow the plan as listed, reading all chapters required and completing the homework, a process that you should already be used to as a student. It is an important step in the education process and in building your financial plan.

High school can be both a positive and challenging period for a young person. My high school years were a mix of both. I gained a lot from my high school experiences, such as a great education, my best friend of twenty eight years, Karey (KD) and an opportunity to be nurtured by some of the best teachers a young man struggling to find his way through life could ever know. I had to grow up rather fast during my high school years (due to personal situations) so I always felt at least three years older than everyone in my class. Along with feeling more mature than the other "kids", I was a very confident person, which most of my classmates didn't understand. In addition to that, I was that quick-witted guy who always had a smart comeback or cutting remark for everything. With that combination going for me, I always got one of two reactions from classmates: they either really liked me or didn't like me at all. Even with all of the highs and lows, I look back on my high school years as some of the best years of my life.

You may look back on your high school years with great joy, see them as a period of your life that you would rather forget, or simply accept them for the mix of experiences that they are. Hopefully, you are enjoying high school more than anything and will look back on these times with fond memories. Whatever the case, take advantage of this opportunity to learn. It may not seem like much of an "opportunity" to you know but it truly is. If asked, most every adult will admit that we would have liked to have been better prepared for college and finances in our junior and senior year of high school.

I can imagine that credit and financial education seems like one more thing we adults are adding to your plate. Well... it is, but for good reason. Although the credit building process may seem like a very "adult" process, it isn't! The following information applies specifically to you, a high school student. Still concerned? Well, let me make one statement that should calm some of your fears: In most cases...**YOU DO NOT NEED TO ESTABLISH CREDIT IN HIGH SCHOOL!** You are a young person whose focus should be on your homework, grades, work, friends and getting ready for college or the workforce. Along with those tasks, you should also begin learning about the credit process and how it works. This information will play a major role in the next phase of your life. Whether you plan to go directly to college, work, trade school, be an entrepreneur, join the military or whatever the case may be, there are steps that you can take in high school that will help you establish good credit and finance habits for your future. The following seven step process will help you advance to the world outside high school AND start the next phase of your life in top credit form!

Step 1

Identify what drives your financial decisions.

Read sessions one and two and do the homework. It is critically important that you pinpoint the internal and external reasons that drive your financial decisions, even as a high school student. Do you have a hard time saving money? Do you plan and budget now? What is the value of money in your life right now? You are now establishing financial habits that will carry you into adulthood. It is highly likely that you will manage your credit the way you currently manage your money; therefore, you want to form good habits while you are young. It doesn't matter whether you have $200 dollars per week or $2 dollars per week. Make sure you are responsible with your finances now! That responsibility begins with understanding yourself FIRST. Make sure you absorb the information and do the homework. Then you'll be ready for step 2.

Step 2

Understand the credit process

Read sessions 3, 7, 8, 9, 11 and 12. These sessions detail the core information regarding credit and the credit process, including; credit reports, credit scores, credit bureaus and etc. It is VITAL that you fully understand the credit process before you can move to step 3. Ask your parents or another responsible adult to explain anything that you don't understand. Refer to the glossary on the website *(www.everythingaboutcredit.com)* to define words that you may not recognize. Make sure you absorb the information and do the homework. Then you'll be ready for step 3.

Step 3

Request your credit report and scores

Once you have fully absorbed the sessions in Step 2, ask your parents (or another responsible adult) to assist you in ordering a copy of your credit reports and scores from the three national credit bureaus. You are allowed one free copy of your credit report each year from each of the big three credit bureaus. The free credit report does not include your credit scores. The credit scores may include a fee; therefore, it is important for you to include your parents or another responsible adult who can help you choose the best option for securing the reports and scores. Each of the big three credit bureaus offer three-in-one credit reports and scores, however, they are generally not free. The free annual credit report provided by the FACTA Act includes individual reports from each of the big three credit bureaus, not the three-in-one version. Please be aware that if you order a three in one credit report and scores, you will only need to order it from one of the credit bureaus. Information for all three credit bureaus will be listed on that one report.

Following are links to the three credit bureaus "free credit report" sites. Feel free to navigate through the sites to access details regarding their free credit report and three-in-one report services.

Equifax:
http://www.equifax.com/answers/request-free-credit-report/en_cp

TransUnion:
http://www.transunion.com/corporate/personal/creditTools/freeCreditReport.page

Experian:
http://www.experian.com/personal-credit/free-credit-report.html

a) Once you have secured your credit report, review its contents for accuracy.

b) Document the date that you received the credit report on the top of the report. This is for your records, as well as being a good barometer of when you need to order your next credit report.

c) If you find no errors on your report, create a file for the credit report (or use an 8 x 10 letter sized envelop). Store the credit report in a locked file cabinet at home or some other safe location (preferably a safe or drawer that has a lock on it). Remember, this report contains ALL of your vital information so it must always be locked in a secure environment!

d) If you find errors on your credit report, identify them by highlighting those entries. You must begin the process of correcting errors and improving negative entries on your credit report. Read Session 14

(Credit Repair and Improvement) and Session 15 (Credit Maintenance) to fully understand the process. If someone has accessed your identity without your knowledge, you will need to begin the process of repairing your credit file now. Also read Session 16 regarding Identity Theft.

Why do you need a credit report if you don't have any credit?

1) The fact is... you don't know what information is listed on your credit reports until you get a copy. With identity theft on the rise, you don't want to wait until you begin applying for college loans to find that someone has used your identity without your knowledge. Remember the young lady I talked about in Session 1 whose mother used the young lady's identity from the age of 13 through 17... unfortunately, it happens. You should secure at least one copy of your credit reports every year starting at age 15 through the remainder of your life! Adults with established credit should get a copy of their credit reports twice per year.

2) You also need a copy of your credit reports to ensure that your vital information is correct. If your social security number is one number off, you may have someone else's information listed on your credit report. Same for your birth date and first and last name. If you and your mother or father have the same name, it is possible that their information may get listed on your credit report accidentally, especially since you may have the same address. Checking your credit regularly is called proactive credit management. It usually takes a significant amount of time to have errors removed or updated on your credit report; therefore, you want to be diligent in ensuring that the information on your credit report is always accurate.

Step 4

Create a budget and savings plan

Remember the sage advice that my generation neglected: Save your money and one day it might save you? This is your opportunity to follow that advice.

Savings Plan:

Create a savings plan that shows specific goals for each quarter (every three months: March, June, September, and December). Setting that goal, reaching it and congratulating yourself helps you see your progress and gain a bit more satisfaction sooner. Establish your plan with weekly deposits. If you can't make weekly deposits, adjust your plan to deposit money every two weeks. Whatever timeframe you use, just make sure you are putting money in your savings account at least twice per month.

Most importantly... remember that a savings plan is just that, for **SAVING**. It is not an emergency fund that you withdraw from when you need new clothes, new hair cut/hairdo, money to "hang out" with your friends or anything else. It is strictly for long-term saving. Your monthly budget should include everything else you need, including emergency funds.

Budget:

Simple advice for every woman and man, start with a pen, a pad and a plan! You should learn to plan and budget early so that it becomes a part of your normal financial routine. Your budget will probably be minor as a young high school student, but the real lesson is learning how to budget. Learning to create and live by a budget will help you through college and as an adult in the workforce. Your weekly budget may include some of the following categories:

- Personal Savings
- Cell Phone
- Food
- Entertainment
- Clothes/Shoes/Personal (i.e.: hair)
- Misc/Emergency

Review your budget and savings plan once per quarter and modify it when needed. Your workbook (or e-book) contains a detailed budget template for your use.

Following these savings and budgeting plans will help you establish critical credit and financial management habits, which include; diligence in saving, sticking to a budget and being a person of your word. These are financial lessons as well as life lessons and character traits that you will use throughout your life.

Step 5

Open a checking and savings account.

Open a savings account by age 14 and include a checking account by age 17. At most major banks; you must be 18 in order to open a checking and savings account by yourself. Ask your
parents or a responsible relative/adult (someone you trust) to open an account with you. They will be the primary person on the account, but you will be equally listed as a joint account holder. BE SURE YOUR PARENTS OR THE RELATIVE/ADULT HAS A POSITIVE FINANCIAL HISTORY WITH THE BANK! If their credit history is not positive, DO NOT ask them to open an account with you. Find another responsible adult that you and your parents trust. I recommend that you DO NOT order checks for your new checking account unless you absolutely need them to pay bills. I also recommend that you do not order a debit card for the account!

Debit card abuse is one of the leading causes of account overages and fee penalties for many adults. The temptation of using a debit card may be a bit overwhelming for an impressionable young person, especially one who may succumb to peer pressure. Begin depositing your savings into the savings account and the money for your budget items into the checking account. Remember to set both accounts up online so you can view and track them electronically.

Step 6

High School Seniors: Change your regular checking account to a "College" checking account at age 18.

At most major banks; you can open a checking and savings account as the primary person at age 18. Many major banks have a "College" checking account. College checking accounts are designed specifically for college students. These accounts do not carry the average minimum balance and fees that regular checking accounts require. They generally do not offer the full array of services (i.e.: no in-bank visits or only a certain number per month) however, it is worth it to not pay the regular service fees. For many college students today, transactions are primarily done online or via ATM anyway. Again, I recommend that you DO NOT order checks for your new checking account unless you absolutely need them to pay bills. If you do order a debit card for your account, I recommend that you leave it at home in a locked, safe environment! The plastic temptation is too strong for many high school seniors.

Step 7

High School Seniors: Be Proactive! Modify your budget and savings plan for college

Your senior year of high school will be a busy time in your life. Modifying your budget and savings plan for college or the workforce will allow you to see exactly kind of expenses you have and what kind of income you require. You may have acquired some monthly expenses by your senior year of high school such as a car and/or phone bill. With those responsibilities come associated expenses. For instance, that car comes with the responsibility of maintenance, gas and car insurance. You may be one of the lucky ones, whose parents pay for your car expenses and maybe even your cell phone. If you are, count your blessings because most teens do not have that luxury, especially in a tough economy. During unsteady economic times, many teens find that they have to foot the bill for many things that their parents simply cannot pay for. That's not necessarily a bad thing though. Making your own way in the world builds character, and gives you a sense of accomplishment that no one can take away.

By January of your senior year (at least five months before graduation), you should have created a sound college budget that includes, at minimum, the following categories:

- Personal Savings
- Gas (Car)
- Car Maintenance
- Car Insurance
- Cell Phone
- Food
- Entertainment
- Clothes/Shoes/Personal (i.e.: hair)
- Misc/Emergency

This updated budget assumes that your college tuition, books, housing and regular meals are taken care of. It may not be a bad idea; however, to add those items to your budget list to get an overall view of your expenses. You will also be able to note when theses expenses are paid, including payment details (date paid, ck number, paid to, etc). The categories on your budget sheet will remain the same each month; however, the budget will change. Remember... you will not need to use each of the categories every month (i.e.: Car Maintenance Clothes/Shoes, etc).

Continue this process and you're on your way!

College Students

And anyone with NO credit

College and young adulthood (18 – 25) are supposed to be two of the great phases of your life. It seems that the best stories are from people's college and young adulthood. It's a time when you are still young enough to believe that you can accomplish anything, but wise enough to know that there are consequences for every decision. This is your first taste of true independence, you're learning to navigate the muddy waters of social and educational networking and you have friends to share it with. It's also usually the time when you begin managing finances independently and that brings about its own set of challenges. Challenges like, not making enough money, not having enough time for school and work, maybe the challenge of a child/family or etc. I just want to tell you that those challenges don't matter! If you are reading this book, no matter what challenges you are having, you are still ahead of the game. This book is designed for the person who wants to educate themselves, manage their finances and create better opportunities for their future. Since you are reading this book, you are obviously that kind of person; therefore, your challenges won't stop you.

Remember this... no matter what comes your way, you are already equipped with everything you need to navigate through those challenges: intelligence, youth, determination and access. You already know that you will be faced with challenges throughout your life. In fact, that's what life is; a series of high, low and in-between experiences that ultimately become your life's journey. A word of advice for you: enjoy the highs and navigate the lows with as much dignity as possible. Develop the skills for proactive life management and problem resolution now. If you do, you will be able to better manage or minimize those challenges. Good credit and financial management skills are a part of that proactive life planning.

Establishing and maintaining good credit has never been as important as it is today. No matter what your plans are after college; workforce, graduate school, the military or etc, you should be establishing and managing your credit while in college. It's especially important now since many employees are requiring credit checks during the hiring process. Why do they require credit checks you ask? Well...young people are beginning to access credit earlier nowadays, sometimes as early as 15/16 years old. Employers want to see if you've established credit and if so, how well you've managed that credit, especially college seniors. Some employers perceive a college senior with good, established credit as a responsible, proactive person who knows how to work within the system. They were wise enough to establish credit early and keep it in good standing. On the other hand, a college senior with no credit or poor credit history may be seen as less responsible in comparison. Employers may see the lack of credit or poor credit as a reflection of their character and conclude that they are more reactive than proactive. Employers should not make these assumptions, however, this is the real world and I can tell you that they often do.

Remember what I said earlier in the book, regarding "perception" playing a large part in the credit process, although it shouldn't. That especially holds true in cases of employment.

This eight step process was designed to help you form good financial management skills and establish credit wisely while in college. It will help you prepare to face the world after graduation with your degree in one hand, great credit report in the other and your eye on future goals... because NOTHING will be holding you back!

******If you have followed this plan from high school, skip to Step 4a and continue from there. If not, start at Step 1.***

Step 1

Identify what drives your financial decisions.

Read sessions one and two and do the homework. It is critically important that you pinpoint the internal and external reasons that drive your financial decisions, even as a high school student. Do you have a hard time saving money? Do you plan and budget now? What is the value of money in your life right now? You are now establishing financial habits that will carry you into adulthood. It is highly likely that you will manage your credit the way you currently manage your money; therefore, you want to form good habits while you are young. It doesn't matter whether you have $200 dollars per week or $2 dollars per week. Make sure you are responsible with your finances now! That responsibility begins with understanding yourself FIRST. Make sure you absorb the information and do the homework. Then you'll be ready for step 2.

Step 2

Understand the credit process

Read sessions 3, 7, 8, 9, 11 and 12. These sessions detail the core information regarding credit and the credit process, including; credit reports, credit scores, credit bureaus and etc. It is VITAL that you fully understand the credit process before you can move to step 3. Ask your parents or another responsible adult to explain anything that you don't understand. Refer to the glossary on the website *(www.everythingaboutcredit.com)* to define words that you may not recognize. Make sure you absorb the information and do the homework. Then you'll be ready for step 3.

Step 3

Request your credit report and scores

Once you have fully absorbed the sessions in Step 2, order a copy of your credit reports and scores from the three major credit bureaus. You are allowed one free copy of your credit report each year from each of the big three credit bureaus. The free credit report does not include your credit scores; however. Be aware that the credit scores may include a fee; therefore, be prepared to pay if required. Each of the big three credit bureaus offer three-in-one credit reports and scores, however, they are generally not free. The free annual credit report provided by the FACTA Act includes reports from each of the big three credit bureaus individually, not the three-in-one version. Please be aware that if you order a three in one credit report and scores, you will only need to order it from one of the credit bureaus. Remember, information for all three credit bureaus will be listed on that one report.

Following are links to the three credit bureaus "free credit report" sites. Navigate through the sites to access details regarding their free credit report and three-in-one report services. Choose the best option for securing the reports and scores.

Equifax:
http://www.equifax.com/answers/request-free-credit-report/en_cp

TransUnion:
http://www.transunion.com/corporate/personal/creditTools/freeCreditReport.page

Experian:
http://www.experian.com/personal-credit/free-credit-report.html

e) Once you have secured your credit report, review its contents for accuracy.

f) Document the date that you received the credit report on the top of the report. This is for your records, as well as being a good barometer of when you need to order your next credit report.

g) If you find no errors on your report, create a file for the credit report (or use an 8 x 10 letter sized envelop). Store the credit report in a locked file cabinet at home or some other safe location (preferably a safe or drawer that has a lock on it). Remember, this report contains ALL of your vital information so it must always be locked in a secure environment!

h) If you find errors on your credit report, identify them by highlighting those entries. You must begin the process of correcting errors and improving negative entries on your credit report. Read Session 14

(Credit Repair and Improvement) and Session 15 (Credit Maintenance) to fully understand the process. If someone has accessed your identity without your knowledge, you will need to begin the process of repairing your credit file now. Also read Session 16 regarding Identity Theft.

Why do you need a credit report if you don't have any credit?

1) The fact is... you don't know what information is listed on your credit reports until you get a copy. With identity theft on the rise, you don't want to wait until you need to access your credit to find that someone has used your identity without your knowledge. Remember the young lady I talked about in Session 1 whose mother used the young lady's identity from the age of 13 through 17... unfortunately, it happens. You should secure at least one copy of your credit reports every year, starting at age 15 through the remainder of your life! Adults with established credit should get a copy of their credit reports twice per year.

2) You also need a copy of your credit reports to ensure that your vital information is correct. If your social security number is one number off, you may have someone else's information listed on your credit report. Same for your birth date and first and last name. If you and your mother or father have the same name, it is possible that their information may get listed on your credit report accidentally, especially since you may have the same address. Checking your credit regularly is called proactive credit management. It usually takes a significant amount of time to have errors removed or updated on your credit report; therefore, you want to be diligent in ensuring that the information on your credit report is always accurate.

Step 4

Remember the sage advice that my generation neglected: Save your money and one day it might save you? This is your opportunity to follow that advice.

Savings Plan:

Create a savings plan that shows specific goals for each quarter (every three months: March, June, September, and December). Setting that goal, reaching it and congratulating yourself helps you see your progress and gain a bit more satisfaction sooner. Establish your plan with weekly deposits. If you can't make weekly deposits, adjust your plan to deposit money every two weeks. Whatever timeframe you use, just make sure you are putting money in your savings account at least twice per month.

Most importantly... remember that a savings plan is just that, for **SAVING**. It is not an emergency fund that you withdraw from when you need new clothes, new hair cut/hairdo, money to "hang out" with your friends or anything else. It is strictly for long-term saving. Your monthly budget should include everything else you need, including emergency funds.

Budget:

Simple advice for every woman and man, start with a pen, a pad and a plan! You should learn to plan and budget early so that it becomes a part of your normal financial routine. Your budget will probably be minor as a young high school student, but the real lesson is learning how to budget. Learning to create and live by a budget will help you through college and as an adult in the workforce. Your weekly budget may include some of the following categories:

- Personal Savings
- Cell Phone
- Food
- Entertainment
- Clothes/Shoes/Personal (i.e.: hair)
- Misc/Emergency

Review your budget and savings plan once per quarter and modify it when needed. Your workbook (or e-book) contains a detailed budget template for your use.

Following these savings and budgeting plans will help you establish critical credit and financial management habits, which include; diligence in saving, sticking to a budget and being a person of your word. These are financial lessons as well as life lessons and character traits that you will use throughout your life.

Step 4a

College Seniors: Update your savings plan and budget for life after college.

You will need to begin balancing your debt and income much more closely as a college senior. You are getting ready to have monthly bills that MUST be paid on time; therefore, you must ensure that your income is sufficient to cover your monthly budget. Your post college monthly budget should, at minimum, have the following categories:

- Personal Savings
- Car Payment (if required)
- Gas (Car)
- Car Maintenance
- Car Insurance
- House/Apartment Payment
- House/Apartment Insurance
- Utilities (Power)
- Utilities (Water)

- Utilities (Gas)
- Utilities (Cable/Internet)
- Credit Card
- School Loan?
- Cell Phone (including phone insurance)
- Food
- Entertainment
- Clothes/Shoes/Personal (i.e.: hair)
- Misc/Emergency

****Your workbook and e-book contains a "College Senior" budget template for your use. Use this template to start your updated budget for life after college.*

Step 5

Open a "College" checking account and a regular savings account.

At most major banks; you can open a checking and savings account as the primary account owner at age 18. Many major banks have a "College" checking account option. College checking accounts are setup specifically for college students. These accounts do not have the average minimum balance and fees associated with them that regular checking accounts require. They generally do not offer the full array of services (i.e.: no in-bank visits or only a certain number per month) however, it is worth it to not pay the regular service fees. For many college students today transactions are primarily done online or via ATM anyway.

Use your own discretion regarding ordering checks for your new account. Do you need checks to pay bills or do you pay bills online or electronically? If you do order checks, I recommend that you do not keep the check book with you at all times. Leave it at home in a locked, safe environment. The same goes for a debit card. You may need access to a debit card at this point in your life. I recommend that you leave the debit card at home in a locked, safe environment! Your budget should allow for any regular and emergency expenses required.

FYI... Debit card abuse is the leading cause of account overages and fee penalties today because many adults are not responsible with debit card use. Unfortunately, a large amount of people do not equate that debit card use to dollars because they don't physically have the cash in hand. If the temptation of using a debit card responsibly is too overwhelming for you...leave the card at home.

Step 6

Juniors... Establish a small amount of credit!

By your junior year of college, you should have established good financial and credit management habits. If you have, you are mature enough to establish and manage a SMALL amount of credit. Small, as a unit of measure, is a relevant term. Therefore, for the sake of this section, let's think of small as: no more than you can afford to pay off with two paychecks. If you gross (or bring home after taxes) $250 per week, you should have no more than $500.00 worth of credit. No matter how much money you make, as a college junior, you should only have between $500 and $1000 maximum worth of credit. Why limit yourself to only $1000 you ask?

As a former college student who was bombarded with credit card offers by my junior year, I understand how easy it is to succumb to the temptation of credit cards. I initially got credit cards for emergencies but was amazing how my life of emergencies suddenly got rather long once I got the credit card. My friends are going to the beach this weekend but I don't have any cash - EMERGENCY. I need to get a really nice birthday present for my girlfriend - EMERGENCY. A group of friends organized a last minute trip to Florida for spring break and I want to go - EMERGENCY. What's interesting is, these emergencies wouldn't have been a passing thought if the credit wasn't available. Do you see what I'm saying?

Following are some of the best ways for you to establish credit. Keep in mind, that you will need some sort of income to take advantage of some of these methods.

- **Ask your parents to include you as an authorized user on their credit account.** *(See the exception for this tip below)*
  One of the long-used methods of helping a college student establish credit was "piggybacking". As noted in Chapter 10, piggybacking allows individuals with bad or no credit to leverage the good payment history of the primary card holder by adding the person's name to an existing credit card account as an authorized user. Parents would sometimes add their college student's name to their credit card account as an authorized user. That would allow the student to "piggyback" on the parent's good credit history; thereby allowing the student to establish credit.

  *****EXCEPTION*****

  Chapter 10 notes that the new FICO 08 and VantageScore credit risk scoring model no longer reports the credit of "authorized users". They will only acknowledge the primary user in these new models; therefore, it won't help students to be added to a credit account as an authorized user under these new models. Therefore, before using this method, have your parents contact their credit card company to determine which scoring model is being used. If they are still using the FICO NextGen model, then your credit will be enhanced by being added as an authorized user. If their credit card company is using one of the new models (FICO '08 or VantageScore) then it will not.

- **Thoroughly understand the credit process and good credit maintenance.**
  Understand debt to income ratio, the importance of paying bills on time, interest rates versus APR rates, and all of the other vital information regarding what actually creates your monthly payments.

- **Establish a checking and savings account with a bank or credit union.**
  Lenders see checking and savings accounts as signs of financial stability and consistent savings behavior. Evidence of responsible, continuous use of checking and savings accounts increase your chances that a lender will offer you credit.

- **Obtain a "Student" credit card from a major bank.**
  Credit Cards are a great way for a college student with no credit to build a credit history. VISA, MasterCard and Discover are just a few of the major lenders who offer their major credit cards specifically designed for college students. Be sure to choose a card with low or nonexistent annual fees and low interest rates. Most importantly, use constraint when choosing your credit limit. Just because a lender offers a certain amount of credit doesn't mean you have to accept it all. If a lender offers $2000 worth of credit, you can simply request $500 of that $2000 be approved.

- **Obtain a SECURED credit card.**
  If you can't get approved for a regular credit card, apply for a secured credit card. With a secured credit card, you are required to deposit money with a lender; your credit limit is usually equal to the deposit. The key to choosing the correct card is to ensure that the card is

reported to the credit bureaus monthly and offers good services and features, such as low to no monthly fees. Not all secured credit card lenders report to the credit bureaus, so be DO YOUR HOMEWORK before choosing your lender.

❖ **Open a department store or gas credit account.**
Open a credit account with a department store or (automobile) gas company. Gas companies and department stores that issue charge cards typically use finance companies, rather than major banks, to handle the transactions. These cards don't do as much for your credit scores as a bank card (Visa, MasterCard, Discover, etc.), but they're usually easier to get. A word of advice to you shop-aholics, do not open an account at your favorite department store; that is too much of a temptation for you. It is best to open an account at a department store that you use, but would not be tempted to over use.

❖ **Get a small installment loan**
Once you have established good saving and spending habits, apply for a small installment loan from a bank or credit union. Please note the words SMALL LOAN. Get a loan that you can pay off within a year, in order to establish good credit before you graduate from college. A one year loan will also limit the amount of interest that you will pay on the loan.

*****EXCEPTION*****

If you obtained a loan in college, you may not want to choose this option. You will have to begin repaying the school loan within six to twelve months of graduation, thereby, establishing loan or installment credit.

Step 7

Always use common sense with your credit... NO EXCUSES!

You must now continuously monitor and manage your credit for the rest of your adult life. Whatever happens with your credit from this point on is **YOUR** responsibility. Letting a friend use your credit card, co-signing for loans for friends or family, taking unexpected trips, unnecessary shopping sprees or allowing random expenses are extremely bad habits to start, and even harder to break once they are established. You are now an adult...no more blaming mom, dad, the dog, the cat, your friends or anyone else for your actions. You are only in control of your credit and finances by controlling your actions. **NO EXCUSES!**

Step 8

Increase your income or cut your budget!

One of the main comments I receive at my seminars for college students is; Mr. Willis, that's good information but I don't have any money. I always tell them that your mentality about financial management has nothing to do with your income. A person who is successful in their financial management is usually successful in their financial mentality. However, I know that college students need income for school and for fun. Here are a few tips for creating, saving and increasing your college income.

- ***Consolidate your student loans***
  Consolidate your student loans at a lower interest rate. This will save you lots of money once you've graduated and begin paying that money back.

- ***Only use student loans to finance your education... NOT YOUR LIFESTYLE!***
  Student loans are for school... not parties or clothes!!!

- ***Buy used books***
  They are much cheaper and contain the same information.

- ***Use your student discount everywhere***
  Always ask if an establishment honors student discounts. Often times restaurants, movie theatres, clothing shops, bookstores honor them but you must ask.

- ***Get a job on campus***
  Library, mailroom, campus coffee shop, etc... the campus is ripe with employment opportunity. Transportation won't be a problem and you will make some extra money.

- ***Adjust your meal plan option***
  If you have a 7 day meal plan but only use it 4 or 5 days, modify that plan and pay less.

- ***Cut back on eating out.***
  Good old cereal and sandwiches are always available and can be made easily. Throw some fruits and vegetables in there for health. FYI...I survived on Top Ramen noodles in college, so I know what I'm talking about.

- ***Limit the amount of weekend "activities" you attend.***
  I know that you are young and want to have fun...and you should. There should be a limit on that when you can't afford it or are spending more money on activities than education.

Homework (Session 13)

Your homework is simple...
FOLLOW THE PLAN EVERY DAY!

That is the only path to success!

Session 14

Credit Repair and Improvement

<u>*How many times have you seen advertisements like these?*</u>

I especially dislike the infomercials that offer instant credit repair and you don't have to lift a finger! And they offer it for the low low price of a few hundred dollars... broken down into three easy payments of course. GIVE ME A BREAK! Why have we not learned by now that nothing good comes that easily and most importantly: if it looks too good to be true, it probably is. Proclamations of instant credit repair or magic credit repair in 30/60/90 days are similar to the boastings of the old sideshow barkers.

Hurry, hurry, step right up. Come one, come all and see the amazingly bad credit history disappear right before your very eyes. Yes it took years to get your credit in this situation, and yes the information is accurate but the feat that I am about to perform will amaze you, dazzle you, put you in a state of total disbelief. I will make this credit history disappear in an instant, all for the low low price of only three hundred dollars ladies and gentleman.

No matter what anyone tells you or sells you, there is no legal method (that I am aware of) to have accurate or inaccurate information removed from your credit history instantly. Most legal, honest and accurate processes for correcting errors take a substantial amount of time.

How Do Credit Report Errors Occur?

Even though most credit bureaus receive monthly updates electronically, someone had to enter the initial information into a system manually. Human interaction causes the risk of human error to be an option from the beginning of the process. One incorrect number entered as your social security number or birth date may turn you into an entirely different person on your credit report. The social security number, birth date and name are reportedly cross checked by the credit bureaus for accuracy but that is clearly not sufficient or all errors would be caught by the credit bureaus. Think about how often you find misspellings of your name or street address on your mail. Then imagine the possibility for error in a report that contains much more information about you. Cases of mistaken identity, stolen identity, out-of-date information, and outright errors can easily occur. Most of your lenders send information to the credit bureaus electronically. If they have an error in their system, they can easily transmit that error to the credit bureaus when they report on your account.

Out of the billions of pieces of data stored in these systems, it is highly likely that you will have errors on your report at some point. The good thing is that you are aware of the potential errors and can proactively review your credit reports. This session will walk you through processes designed to help you correct and improve information in your credit file. These processes will require hands on management, thorough dedication and unwavering persistence on your part. It will not happen overnight and most of all it will require patience, but you can do this!

The Dispute Process

Disputing credit entries is one of the primary processes you will use to correct errors on your credit report. The dispute process is used in conjunction with other repair and improvement processes. I will review the dispute process, in detail, before diving into specific repair/improvement related topics. Disputing a credit entry alone may not remove the error from your credit file; however, it is the first step to beginning the process.

People often make the mistake of contacting the credit bureau when they find an error in their credit file. That actually isn't the best course of action in most cases. Remember that the credit bureau is simply entering information into your credit file that creditors have reported to them. When you find errors in your personal information from the credit bureau (name, address, SS#, birth date, etc) you should process a dispute with the credit bureau to have it corrected. When you find errors on your credit report regarding a specific credit account, you should report it to the specific lender first. The creditor should check/update their records and notify all of the credit bureaus of the updates within 30 days. That's what's supposed to happen. As we all know; however, there are many things in life that don't happen as they are supposed to. Therefore, you need to be proactive and manage the situation until it is resolved. Don't leave it to the creditor to contact the credit bureaus; you should do that as a part of your credit management process.

Following are the proper steps to take upon finding errors on your credit report:

1) Contact the lender
Verify that your account is in good standing with the lender and correct any errors in the account status. For instance, if your credit card company has an inaccurate late payment entry on your credit report, contact the credit card company first so they can update their files.

2) Secure a copy of your updated account file
Once the error has been corrected, request an updated copy of your account file from your creditor, either by mail or online. You will need this account file as supporting documentation for your dispute with the credit bureaus.

3) Ask the lender to update the credit bureaus
Lenders are required to update your file with each of the credit bureaus once an error is identified and updated; however, you should not rely on that. Once you verify that your account is in good standing, ask the lender to update their information with the credit bureaus. It is the

lender's responsibility to report accurate information to the credit bureaus.

4) File a dispute with the credit bureaus

Do not assume that the creditor will contact the credit bureaus right away or at all. File a dispute with each of the credit bureaus right away in order to begin the process of having the inaccurate information updated in your credit file. Once you have filed the dispute with the credit bureaus, they will begin their own investigation as well.

5) Send a copy of your dispute and supporting documentation to the lender.

Yes, I know this sounds a bit redundant; nonetheless, you must ensure that the lender updates the credit bureaus. The mailed information (with a return receipt request) will jog the lender's memory if they have not already updated your file with the credit bureaus. Lenders are also aware that you can file a complaint with the FTC (Federal Trade Commission) if they do not comply when an error is found.

Once the dispute is filed with the credit bureaus, they are required to investigate, per each credit bureaus standards of investigation. Each credit bureau will then provide you with a free, updated credit file within 30 to 60 days of your filing date that reflects the results of their individual investigations. The credit bureau's basic investigation process includes contacting the lender to verify the accuracy of the entry in your credit report. There is also the possibility of the credit bureaus sending only part of the detailed dispute information to lenders, which may make it more difficult for lenders to resolve the issue. Again, that is why it is vital that you contact the lender first. Upon completion of the credit bureau's investigation, the entry will either be updated, removed or remain as is, based upon each credit bureau's investigation results and standards. The credit bureaus must remove entries if lenders do not respond within the required investigation period.

Be aware that lenders can put the entry back in your credit file during the next reporting cycle. Many consumers who have filed disputes report and had erroneous information removed also noted that the entry reappeared during the next reporting cycle. Under the Fair and Accurate Credit Transactions Act (FACTA), if negative information is removed as a result of a consumer's dispute, it may not be reinserted without notifying the consumer within five days, in writing. This is a shining example of why you must remain diligent about your credit management. Check your credit report 30, 60 and 90 days after an erroneous entry is removed to ensure that it does not reappear.

Online and Manual Dispute Processes

Each of the big three credit bureaus list detailed processes on their website regarding filing a dispute and correcting credit report errors. Please visit each website for specific information regarding online and manual dispute processes. Following is an overview of the general dispute process, including contact information for each of the three credit bureaus.

Online Dispute:

1) What websites do I access for an online dispute?

Equifax:

http://www.equifax.com/answers/correct-credit-report-errors/en_cp

TransUnion:

http://annualcreditreport.transunion.com/entry/disputeonline

Experian:

http://www.experian.com/disputes2/index.html

2) What can you dispute online?
Credit accounts, bankruptcies, collections, liens, inquiries, judgments and personal identification information.
(Check each credit bureau's website for their specific list of disputes allowed online)

3) What kind of supporting documents can I use to support claims for errors?

a. Personal Information Change *(name, address, etc)*
- Updated drivers licenses
- Updated social security card
- Marriage certificate/Divorce decree

b. Account History/Public Records
- Updated account statement from lender
- Official identity theft documentation

(Check each credit bureau's website for their specific list of supporting documentation required)

4) What information do you need?
b. A recent copy of your individual credit reports
c. Three copies of supporting documents to confirm your dispute *(do not send originals)*
d. Online dispute form *(from each credit bureau)*
e. Dispute letter/email summarizing your claim

5) How do I check the status of my dispute online?
Access the websites listed on the previous page to check the status of your dispute online. Each credit bureau uses different criteria for checking the status of a dispute. Some credit bureaus use your credit report number; some assign a specific number to you after the dispute is filed. Use the specific code or number as instructed by each credit bureau's website, to check the status of your dispute online.

You should also know that:

- ❖ In most cases, if you submit your dispute online the results of the investigation will only be provided to you online.

- ❖ While the dispute investigation is in progress, the account will be noted as ***"In Dispute"*** on your credit report. This will not change the entry on your report or the status of the account however.

- ❖ Within 30 days of your filing, the credit bureaus should send email notification of the status of its investigation online. The final status of the dispute will be changed once the investigation is completed if required.

- ❖ You should forward a copy of your completed credit bureau dispute form and supporting documents to the lender after you've completed your dispute with the credit bureaus.

Manual Dispute:

You will need to complete the credit bureau's specific dispute form for most manual disputes. Please have the form downloaded from each website or contact each credit bureau directly to request a copy of their dispute form and instructions for filing a manual dispute.

1) What address and phone number do I access for a manual dispute?

Equifax:

Equifax Credit Information Services, Inc.
P.O. Box 740241
Atlanta, GA 30374
Equifax Dispute Line: (800) 685-1111

TransUnion:

TransUnion Consumer Solutions
P.O. Box 2000
Chester, PA 19022-2000
TransUnion Dispute Line: (800) 916-8800

Experian:

PO Box 2002
Allen, TX 75013
Consumer Credit Questions
Experian Dispute Line: (888) 397-3742

2) What can you dispute manually?

Credit accounts, bankruptcies, collections, liens, inquiries, judgments and personal identification information.
(Check each credit bureau's website for their specific list of disputes allowed online)

3) What kind of supporting documents can I use to support claims for errors?

a. Personal Information Change *(name, address, etc)*

- Updated drivers licenses
- Updated social security card
- Marriage certificate/Divorce decree

b. Account History/Public Records

- Updated account statement from lender
- Official identity theft documentation
-

(Check each credit bureau's website for their specific list of supporting documentation required)

4) What information do you need?

a. A recent copy of your individual credit reports
b. Three copies of supporting documents to confirm your dispute *(do not send originals)*

c. Online dispute form *(from each credit bureau)*
d. Dispute letter/email summarizing your claim

5) How do I check the status of my dispute manually?
Contact each credit bureau via the phone numbers listed on the pages 163 and 164 to check the status of your dispute manually. Each credit bureau uses different criteria for checking the status of a dispute. Some credit bureaus use your credit report number; some assign a specific number to you after the dispute is filed. Use the specific code or number as instructed by each credit bureau's website, to check the status of your dispute online.

FYI...

❖ Generally, the status of manual disputes are received via phone or fax.

❖ In most cases, if you submit your dispute manually the results of the investigation will only be provided to you manually.

❖ While the dispute investigation is in progress, the account will be noted as ***"In Dispute"*** on your credit report. This will not change the entry on your report or the status of the account however.

❖ Within 30 days of your filing, the credit bureaus should send manual notification of the status of its investigation. The final status of the dispute will be changed once the investigation is completed, if required.

❖ You should mail a copy of your completed credit bureau dispute form and supporting documents to the lender after you've completed your dispute with the credit bureaus.

Don't Forget...
Mail or fax copies (not originals) of your completed dispute form and supporting documentation to the credit bureaus as well as the creditor. Be sure to include a return receipt request for verification of receipt.

Dispute Letter/Email Samples

It is always a good idea to put your detailed issues in writing, and especially so in this case. Writing your own, detailed letter to creditors, gives them thorough information to help resolve the issue and offers insight into any additional circumstances. Your workbook contains several sample dispute letters and phone scripts for your use. Feel free to modify these letters when resolving issues with creditors and the credit bureaus.

**The following information assumes that you have a recent copy of your credit reports.*

Correcting personal information errors

Your personal information is sensitive information that identifies and distinguishes you from any other consumer, such as:

a) Your current name and former name (s)
b) Your social security number
c) Your current address and previous addresses
d) Your phone number
e) Your date of birth
f) Your current employer and previous employers

Although there is no third party investigation required, you must still use the dispute process to correct personal information errors. Following are instructions for correcting personal information errors:

1) Access a recent copy of your credit report.
2) Make a copy of your updated driver's license, social security card or any other supporting documentation that supports your claim.
3) Contact the creditor to update your personal information.
4) Contact each credit bureau, via their dispute process, to update the incorrect personal information.
5) Attach a custom dispute letter/email with your information and mail copies to each credit bureau.
6) Check your monthly states and verify that all of your lenders have the correct information as well.

You should receive an updated credit report from each of the credit bureaus no later than 60 days after the dispute has been filed. The updated report will reflect the details of the investigations by the credit bureaus.

Correcting inaccurate account information
(Account History and Public Records)
It has been reported that almost 13 million consumers find inaccuracies on their credit reports each year. If you are diligent in regular credit maintenance, it is highly likely that you will find inaccurate information on your credit report over your lifetime. You must; however, be as diligent about monthly financial management, which includes reviewing your detailed bills every month. Many issues with the credit bureau can be circumvented by simply identifying the error on your monthly billing statement and correcting it before it is reported to the credit bureau.

The Fair Credit Billing Act include built-in protection for consumers who find billing errors on their monthly billing statements. The consumer must contact the lender in writing within 60 days of receiving the incorrect bill. The creditor must respond to the notice within 30 days and cannot damage the consumer's credit rating while the item is in dispute. Under the FCRA, a creditor cannot report a consumer's (revolving credit) account as delinquent, when that consumer is disputing a charge.

Following is the process for disputing inaccurate credit information on your credit report:

1) Secure a copy of your credit report.
2) Contact the creditor to dispute the inaccurate information.
3) Obtain a copy of your corrected account file from your creditor.
4) Ask the creditor to update their file with the credit bureaus immediately.
5) File a dispute with each of the credit bureaus, per their individual dispute processes. Attach a custom dispute letter/email with your completed dispute.
6) Send a **copy** of your completed dispute form, dispute letter and all supporting documentation to your creditor.
7) Check the status of your dispute within 30 days for an update.
8) Once the issue has been corrected, check your credit report in another 60 days to verify that the item hasn't reappeared on your credit report.

You should receive an updated credit report from each of the credit bureaus no later than 90 days after the dispute has been filed. The updated report will reflect the details of the investigations by the credit bureaus.

Improving negative (accurate) account information

(Account History and Public Records)

I mentioned this earlier, but it bears repeating: the primary way to repair factual, damaging credit information is to wait. Despite anyone's claims of miracle credit repair, there is little you can do to remove negative entries if the information is accurate. The FCRA (Fair Credit Reporting Act) requires that such information remain on your credit report for seven years, with several exceptions: bankruptcies may remain on your report for ten years and lawsuit-related information may remain until the suit is settled. Your best bet for avoiding these credit problems is prevention: pay your bills on time and manage your credit diligently.

Although you may not be able to erase negative entries from your credit report, there are some things that you can do to help minimize the impact of these entries and improve your credit score in the meantime.

a) Verify your personal information

Make sure that your personal information (i.e.: name, address, social security number, date of birth, etc.) are correct on your credit report. A small mistake like having one incorrect number in your birth date or social security number can allow someone else's credit information to be entered on your report.

b) Make a statement

If a dispute was not resolved to your satisfaction, you have the right to add a 100 word personal statement to your credit file. 100 words may be a bit brief for your statement; therefore, you must simply use your words wisely and stick to the facts when creating your statement. Please be aware that the personal statement does not change the status of your negative entry, neither does it change your credit score itself. It simply gives the creditor an opportunity to read any underlying facts regarding the entry. Use those hundred words to clarify inaccuracies or specify details. It is not a forum to complain about your boss cutting your hours making you unable to pay on time or any other frivolous reason for your delinquency. Remember that everyone who requests a copy of your credit report will also receive your statement. The credit bureau does not take the statement into consideration; however a lender may read it, which may in turn trigger other questions during their investigation. There is no guarantee that the statement will make any difference to the investigation; however, it's worth including, just in case it does.

c) Pay off Any Collection Accounts less than two years old!

When creditors essentially give-up on collecting payments for a past due account they hire a collection agency to retrieve the balance owed on the account or they simply sell the account to a collection agency. This puts that account in "Collections" status on your credit report. Paying off accounts that are in collection (including charge offs) may not immediately increase your credit score, but it will show potential lenders that you have taken care of your financial responsibility on that account. Collection accounts cause major damage to your credit report, as they are calculated in the Payment History portion of most credit scoring models.

The Payment History portion accounts for the largest section of most credit scoring models; thereby carrying the most weight when calculating your score. A large number of points are instantly removed from your credit score when a collection account is listed on your credit file. Other lenders see this as a red flag as well. When potential lenders are judging the likelihood of your repaying a debt as promised, they see collection accounts as evidence that you have not been responsible enough to do so in the past, therefore, they may not extend credit to you.

Be aware that many lenders only focus on the last two years of your credit history. Therefore, you should focus on any open collection accounts that are less than two years old. Collection accounts remain on your credit report seven years from the "date of last activity", not the date that it was initially reported, like many other entries. That means the collection account can remain on your credit report seven years from the last date that the creditor reported the account. Here are your options for improving collection accounts:

1) Pay the collection account in full.

2) Make arrangements to pay the balance in installments. (Be aware that lenders are often reluctant to agree to monthly payments for collection accounts, given the fact that you did not honor the original monthly payment agreement)

3) Negotiate a settlement amount. (Read ahead for details on negotiating a settlement)

d) Negotiate a settlement!

Some creditors will negotiate reduced payoff amounts for accounts in collections. Simply call the lender to negotiate a lower payoff or a "settlement" amount. Lenders are under no obligation to negotiate a settlement amount; however, lenders would rather get a partial payment than no payment, so it's worth a try. Your workbook and e-book includes negotiation notes and sample scripts. Read the notes for additional instruction on negotiating settlements and customize the scripts for your negotiations.

Here are some tips to help you with your negotiations.

Negotiation Tips:

1) Construct your plan!
Document your negotiation plan and customize your negotiation script and information to fit each company's profile.

2) Know your price and start low!
Before you start calling creditors, determine how much you can afford to pay them and identify your high point (i.e.: 50% of the total debt). The lender will more than likely counter whatever you offer; therefore, begin negotiations 20% lower than your high point. Put that information in your negotiation plan so that you will not agree to pay more than your set high point.

3) Know your timeline!
Define how long it will take you to pay off the amount you agree on in the increments specified, if required. Repeat this information to the creditor several times before completing your negotiations.

4) Be persistent!
If the first person will not negotiate with you, ask to speak with someone else, then a manager. Most companies would rather receive some money than none.

5) Be aware!
Some companies do not accept installment payments on accounts that have been negotiated for less than is owed. Be ready to pay the full negotiated amount on the date or within the timeframe promised.

6) Act Fast!
Companies have no obligation to negotiate a settlement price! Take advantage of account settlement opportunities when they arise.

7) Know your environment!
You are attempting to have a legitimate debt decreased. The creditor is probably not going to be happy about this. Research the company's policies as much as possible before beginning your negotiation.

8) Negotiate fees and updates!
Make the removal of late fees and the update of your credit bureau entry a part of your negotiation. If they will not agree to forgive the fees you should not budge until they agree to have the negative entry removed or at minimum updated to show "Paid As Agreed" in your credit file. *(Be aware that it is much easier to get lenders to agree to remove the negative credit report entry if you offer to pay the entire negotiated amount in full rather than in installments)*

9) Verify EVERYTHING!
Document the conversation, including the final negotiated terms while you are on the phone with the creditor. This includes the person's name, title, direct number, email address, manager, date of call, time of call, etc. Review the final details with the lender twice before completing the call.

10) Get the letter!
Ask the lender to forward an official agreement letter that details your final negotiations, within 24 to 48 hours of your conversation. Verbally inform them that if everything agreed upon is not in the letter you will not honor the agreement as well as stating that in a follow-up email. Most importantly, DO NOT SEND ONE PENNY until you receive that letter. When you send the payment, include a

copy of the agreement letter as well.

Use the negotiation script samples in your workbook and e-book to help craft your personal negotiation script. Customize your negotiation scripts and techniques for each lender and remember to be persistent.

Improving negative (accurate) account information... continued

e) Separate your credit

Spouses have the option of having their credit histories listed separately, including joint accounts. A spouse can also remove their name from a joint account by requesting the update and/or changing their (last name). Married women can exercise their option of using their birth name or married name. These options sometimes allow your credit score to be raised. Remember that the credit scoring model simply takes into account vital information, name, address, SS#, birth date and etc, when identifying a consumer. It does not connect all factors of a person's history.

f) Pay your credit cards down

First things first...LIMIT YOUR CREDIT CARD USAGE! Get a handle on your spending first or all of your efforts to increase your credit score are simply wasted! Pay all credit cards and credit accounts down to at least 50% of your available credit. I always recommend keeping it down to 40% of the available credit for safety sake; however, your minimum should be 50%. Your credit score is automatically lowered when you use over 50% of your available credit. Credit card payments are accounted for in the Payment History section in most credit scoring models. Payment History makes up the largest portion of your credit score calculation. Therefore, it is very important to manage your credit cards diligently and keep the balances down to at least 50% of the available credit.

Be sure to pay, at minimum, the minimum monthly payment on your credit cards to remain in good standing: however, most credit cards will never get paid in full by paying the minimum payment amount. Even if you pay the full minimum monthly payment owed each month, the outstanding balance percentage has an impact on your score. When financial institutions review your credit report, they calculate the possibility of you using all of the available credit on your credit cards and factor-in the monthly payments that would be required to service that debt. Create a plan to pay double the minimum payment amount, preferably more every month. If required, secure additional income through a part-time job. Commit the income from that part-time job to paying your credit cards down or in full. I had to do it as a young adult so I know that it's not easy; but trust me; it's worth it in the end.

g) Raise your credit card limit

Raising your credit limit is a bit more difficult than it was a few years ago. In fact, when advising clients one-on-one, I first suggest that they pay their credit cards down to 40% of their available credit before raising their credit card limit. If you possess the self control to raise your credit limit and not access the new credit it, raising your credit card limit by 50% may be an option for you. If you don't have the will power to increase the credit card limit and not utilize the additional credit then you are only adding to your problems. It is very important that you see the additional credit as a band-aid with the goal being to get the credit card balance down to 50% of your available credit limit.

h) Diversify the types of credit that you have

It is important that you diversify the types of credit that you have to accommodate the new credit models. The new models not only verify that you have a credit history; it drills down to the types of credit you have. This, supposedly, demonstrates your responsibility with various types of credit. If you have several of the same types of credit accounts (i.e.: major credit cards, department stores, etc.) then you may want to pay some of those off and not use them (but don't cancel them). You should then apply for a small amount of (i.e.: revolving credit) in order to diversify the type of credit that you have.

i) Correct Identity Theft Issues

Identity theft is a major issues today. If you've been a victim of identity theft and it affects your credit, there are things that you can do to correct this. Chapter sixteen offers detailed information regarding preventing identity theft and repairing damage done by identify theft, so I won't go into any detail in this section. The best thing you can do; however is to be proactive! Put some sort of preventative measure in place for your credit AND debit cards BEFORE you become a victim. Many banks offer a purchase verification services and daily limits on credit and debit cards. These services require verbal verification for purchases over a pre-determined amount on credit and debit transactions. For example, if you put a $500 daily cap on your credit or debit cards, the bank would approve up to $500 dollars worth of purchases in one day and would require verbal verification, including a pre-defined password from you to approve any additional purchases. This service actually saved me from a potentially crushing financial setback when my credit card was stolen and used.

j) Beware of Dishonest Credit REPAIR Agencies

Every adult should take the time to research and choose the credit improvement option that works best for them. I am neither recommending nor dissuading you from using a credit repair agency. That being said, I do not advocate the use of credit repair agencies that make claims of repairing or erasing bad credit. Many of these agencies charge a fee to simply dispute negative information on your behalf and some of them attempt to negotiate settlement deals with your creditors...all things that you can do for yourself. In addition, some credit repair agencies promise all kinds of miracles when their primary tool for "fixing" your credit is to ultimately have you file for bankruptcy. I have heard some of the most outlandish and illegal tactics used by some of the more nefarious credit agencies over the last 20 years. The bottom line is this... you will be the one who chooses whether or not to hire a third party credit service, so you should make sure you research every organization that you are considering thoroughly. After all, you will make the decision and you will deal with the results of that decision.

k) Consider a Credit Counseling Service

If you choose to use an outside service to help you improve your credit, I suggest using one of the "not for profit" credit counseling services. These credit counselors are generally a part of the National Foundation for Credit Counseling (NFCC) and can be contacted through their website: www.nfcc.com. Credit counseling services generally offer more hands-on, financial management services, in addition to credit improvement advice. If they charge a fee, many offer a sliding scale fee for services. To learn out about organizations in your area that help consumers improve their credit scores and assist with hands-on financial management, contact the National Foundation for Credit Counseling.

National Foundation for Consumer Credit
8611 Second Avenue
Silver Spring, MD 20910
http://www.nfcc.org
800-388-2227
800-682-9832 (Spanish)

l) Alternate Credit Repair Options

Debt Consolidation and Bankruptcy were widely regarding as viable options for credit and finance improvement before the credit crisis of 2007. Needless to say, things are quite different in 2009. Credit isn't so readily available to the average consumer, as banks are not lending as easily as they did in previous years. In addition, creditors are cutting credit limits to reduce consumer's available credit thereby reducing the company's own credit liability. People are finding that certain credit cards, revolving and installment credit limits have been ceremoniously reduced without them even being notified; some by up to 50%. Following is high level information regarding both options; however, I advise you to speak with a professional financial advisor and bankruptcy attorney before considering debt consolidation or bankruptcy as options

Debt consolidation

Debt consolidation is still an option for some people, especially those with a good amount of equity in their homes and a good credit score. Be aware, however, that the process for securing cash or a line of credit for equity in your home may be a bit more difficult to acquire, given the caution that banks are now using. There are options out there for those with equity in their homes. I suggest that you go online and check (interest and APR) rates and requirements for your bank, your credit union and an alternate bank before submitting an application. If you are not comfortable with your knowledge of this process please consult with a bank or licensed financial professional for your best options.

Bankruptcy *(Chapter 7, 11 and 13)*

My general rule of thumb regarding bankruptcy is: exhaust ALL resources for debt repayment before considering bankruptcy. I am aware that many people are finding themselves considering bankruptcy as an option now and I wouldn't dare begin to give you advice on bankruptcy in the pages of this book. That kind of advice would have to come from an advisor who has reviewed your financial situation in detail. I am sure that anyone who has had to file bankruptcy did so as a last ditch effort to repair their financial outlook, and I understand that. I would; however, advise anyone considering bankruptcy to consult with an experienced financial advisor and bankruptcy attorney first. The financial advisor will first review your current financial status and recommend steps to improve your situation outside bankruptcy (if there are any) and the attorney would advise you of the legal ramifications of a bankruptcy. If you feel that bankruptcy is an option, please consult these professionals as they help you choose the best possible option for you and your family.

How long will it take to improve my credit?

You should think of your credit repair journey as a long-term process. Improving bad credit will take time so you must be patient. The length of time it takes depends on your current credit situation. As you follow good credit rules such as paying your bills on time, paying collection accounts and etc., your credit score will slowly increase. In this respect, time is your friend and your enemy... in a sense. Remember that there is a statute of limitations for most negative items. Most negative items can only stay on your credit report for seven years. If you do absolutely nothing (pay debt and avoid using credit) then your scores are going to slowly improve over time.

As negative items get older, their value is going to diminish and the credit scores will start to improve. As I stated previously, some lenders only focus on the last two years of your credit history anyway. So make sure your credit improvement plan focuses on the last two years of your credit history first. Whichever route you choose, the credit repair process will take time and diligence, but it will be worth it to see those credit score numbers continuously rise!

Homework (Session 14)

It's time to put your reading into action!
Let's make that score go up, up, up!

Complete the homework for Session 14 in your workbook or e-book.

Session 15

Credit Maintenance

I often wonder why we put more emphasis on credit repair than credit management. Isn't that putting the proverbial cart before the horse? One reason may be because the credit repair industry is a big money industry... scam artists and opportunist are more aware of that than anyone. That is why we should require students to complete at least one credit and finance course per year beginning in their sophomore year of high school through their senior year of high school. That way, teens will have a good idea of how the credit and finance system works, the latest changes each year and most importantly, how to best manage their money and maintain their good credit score by the time they leave high school.

If you're saying Brian, since this is your bright idea, why don't YOU make that happen, I say to you... good response! Actually... I am working to make this happen. I'm currently working to have a credit and finance course offered in several private schools and hope to eventually expand it to public schools. I am even donating my time for this goal because I believe it will help many young people find the path to financial freedom early in life.

When I speak to high school students about credit and finance, I often use the analogy of a 16 year old being handed the keys to a brand new car and allowed to drive before ever taking one driver's class. They may be of legal age to operate a vehicle and they may know a little about operating the vehicle, but they have no idea what to expect on the road because they didn't learn the rules. He or she will inevitably have issues because they were not educated before they acted. Many of us full-fledged adults would have appreciated a class in credit and finance when we were teenagers, but that's water under the bridge. Luckily, you were wise enough to buy my book and educate yourself, and if you're the parent of a teenage, I hope you pass it along to them as well. Better yet, buy them a copy of their own.

By this point in the book, you should be aware that credit maintenance is VITAL! Whether you are in the process of establishing credit, repairing credit or simply managing your credit, it is important that you integrate consistent credit maintenance into your regular financial management routine. This will keep your good accounts in good standing and will establish good maintenance habits when your negative entries have improved. Make sure you understand the factors that affect your credit and make a personal commitment to properly manage your credit. Maintaining your credit score will prove to be invaluable throughout your life. It will also help you in many aspects of your life outside your finances. When you're not worried about your finances it frees your mind to think about more productive, progressive things. Anything that offers you that kind of peace of mind is priceless.

Following are some basic tips for good credit maintenance. Some of these credit maintenance tips have been mentioned throughout the book, but they bear repeating.

1. Check your credit report at least twice per year!

I've said this one hundred times but it's worth repeating a

hundred more: get your credit report and scores at least twice per year...once per year minimum! With the rise in identity theft and erroneous reporting, you don't want to leave anything up to chance. This process should be integrated into your regular financial management plan as well as being listed on your financial calendar.

2. Make a budget and stick to it!

You will never get a handle on your credit if you do not have a handle on your overall financial management. Create a monthly budget that includes all of your monthly income and expenses. Most importantly stick to your budget and do not allow yourself to overspend or open accounts that you will not be able to repay. Many credit issues can be avoided by using wise financial management. Making a budget and sticking to it will be one of the smartest decisions you will ever make

3. Pay your bills on time!

Pay ALL of your bills on time all the time! This is a simple statement that can help you avoid years of credit issues. Remember that every on time payment will affect your credit history positively. If you can pay more than the required amount, do so, especially on accounts with balances. Consider setting up automatic payments or paying your bills online as an option. Also, use restraint in creating bills. As the saying goes, "don't do the crime if you can't do the time". Don't take on bills that you can't pay no matter how badly you want the item. That desire for the item will pass in a few moments; an unpaid debt lingers on your credit report for years.

4. Limit your credit card spending!

Avoid using credit cards to make purchases that you can't afford! Credit cards allow easy access to items that you would normally not be able to purchase. Keep in mind; however, that with every swipe of your card you are increasing your debt! Weigh the risk when deciding whether you **need** an item or simply **want** the item. Remember our needs/wants review from Session 1? Before every purchase, ask yourself, is this item going to add value to my life, my assets or will it be a liability to my budget? Credit card is easy to get into but very hard to get out of, so avoid it at any cost.

5. Pay no less than your minimum monthly payment on your credit card balances!

Always pay, at least, the minimum monthly payment on your credit card balances; however, I recommend doubling that whenever possible. Paying your minimum balance every month shows creditors that you are responsible enough to honor your agreement of payment. It keeps your credit in good standing and gives you more options where credit is concerned. Doubling your payments help you pay the card down quicker.

6. Keep your credit card balances below 50% of your available credit amount!

Another running theme throughout this book is regarding your credit card balances being kept below 50% of your available credit amount. Keeping your credit card balances below 50% of your available credit keeps your credit score intact. Keeping it below 40% allows you another 10% of fluctuation before hitting the 50% mark (hint hint). The moment that your credit card balance goes to 51% of your available balance, your credit score is automatically lowered.

7. Pay outstanding balances as soon as possible!

Outstanding balances weigh heavily on your credit score, as they factor into your Payment History. Payment history is the largest portion of most credit scoring models. Outstanding balances and late payments are generally rated on a 30 day rotation. At 30 days late, you are generally reported to the credit bureaus and your score is automatically affected. Your score is affected with every 30 day rotation afterwards (60/90/120 days). Pay any late or outstanding balances right away in order to keep your credit score in tact or to improve your score.

8. Do not close old accounts.
Closing old accounts reduces your credit history. Having a substantial credit history benefits your score, especially if that history is good. Pay off any open accounts that carry a balance and are less than two years old, especially collection or charge-off accounts, but don't close them.

9. Limit the amount of credit accounts that you open.
Remember that the numbers of credit accounts you have in comparison to your income (Debt to Income) are a major factor for lenders when deciding to grant or deny credit. Your debt to income ratio is always a factor when applying for new credit. When your debit to income ratio is too high it causes your credit score to be lowered and makes it harder for you to attain new credit.

10. Avoid shopping for credit
Applying for numerous new credit accounts will negatively affect your score. Each inquiry can shave up to 6 points from your overall credit score. In addition, too many inquiries can signal to a potential lender that you're a risky prospect. Remember that Hard Inquiries affect your credit score; however, Soft Inquiries do not. (See Session 11 for details)

11. Stay within the same occupation as long as possible
Although your credit score is one of the primary factors that creditors look at when reviewing your credit history, it is not the only factor. Some creditors also take your job or occupation, length of employment and whether you own a home into consideration as well.

12. Review your monthly bill statements thoroughly
Ever hear the saying "the devil is in the details", well the fine print is where all of the details lie when it comes to monthly billing statements. Read your monthly billing statements thoroughly in order to catch any new changes or updated policies. Make sure you receive a copy of all your monthly bills electronically or by mail. Review them thoroughly each month... including the fine print.

14. Diversify the types of credit that you have
It is important that you diversify the types of credit that you have to accommodate the new credit models. The new models not only verify that you have a credit history; it drills down to the types of credit that you have established. This, supposedly, demonstrates your responsibility with the various types of credit.

15. Keep an eye on your credit accounts!
Many people are finding their credit limits on credit cards and various other credit accounts being reduced at the lender's whim. What's more, some lenders are not informing consumers before making these changes. Several clients have contacted me recently about credit card and finance companies cutting their credit limits in half. This is a major problem because if you are keeping your balance down to 50% of your available credit limit, having it cut by even 10% puts you under the 50% limit, which sends your credit score plummeting! Review your monthly statements thoroughly. That is often the first indication you have of any changes to your credit line.

Your credit status is not static; it can change on a whim, which is why you must be diligent in managing and protecting it. Having the access to credit is, at times, more important than exercising that access. Like most things in life, you should have the option of credit, and the primary way to keep that option in tact is to keep your credit score as high as possible. Credit is a privilege, not a right. Every time you buy something on credit it's the same as taking out a loan. Be proactive in your credit and financial management and maintenance. This will allow you to enjoy all of the benefits that good credit allows.

FYI...

Did you know that more independent merchants are beginning to use collection agencies to collect unpaid debt? Most people are aware that they will be reported to a collection agency for unpaid credit card or automobile debt; however, not many people are aware that your credit can now suffer for an unpaid parking ticket, lost or overdue library book, unreturned video/DVD rental, speeding ticket or health club membership. Collection agencies are being hired to "track down" delinquencies and non-payments and are quickly reporting them to at least one of the big three credit bureaus. Be diligent, be responsible and be aware!

Homework (Session 15)

Maintaining your credit will be the most important task of all!

Complete the homework for Session 15 in your workbook or e-book.

Session 16

Identity Theft

Fraud, Scam and Theft. Unfortunately, many of us have had to deal with this reality at some point in our lives. I include myself in the "us" category because I was a victim of identity theft in 2007. Someone stole my VISA card number and spent almost $1000 dollars at various stores in New Jersey. They would have gotten more but I have an alert on my credit cards that capped the dollar amount they had access to. The incident was incredibly baffling to me.

I was at home in North Carolina with my VISA card safely tucked away in my wallet when I was notified by my bank that they had frozen my account due to "suspicious transactions". The thief obviously secured my credit card number and vital information and somehow used it at two retail locations in New Jersey. My bank reissued the stolen credit within 24 hours as part of their identity theft guarantee but I was quite disturbed by this. The proactive notification alert that I put on my credit cards saved me from a potentially devastating financial situation. I've heard stories where people have had their lives ruined due to identity theft. It took some of them years to straighten out the mess that thieves caused. You should be as proactive as possible when it comes to protecting your identity, credit and personal information. We live in a highly electronic age... even our money is primarily electronic. It's extremely important that we protect ourselves, as much as possible, from the myriad of fraudulent people, websites and organizations that are simply covers for credit fraud, scams and identity theft.

Many of us make purchases online on a regular basis. It is equally important for us to ensure that our information is being processed over a secure line. Studies show that you are probably safer entering your information over a secure line than you are giving your credit card to a cashier at a store. The cashier could easily record your credit card number, name and authorization code and order product online quite easily. All they would need is your address, which they could easily ascertain by asking to see your driver's license... for identification purposes of course. That is why you should take precautions every time you use your credit card. Also be careful of how you dispose of bills and documents that contain private and vital information. Be proactive by protecting your information at all times.

What is Identity Theft?

Identity theft is a broad label that includes many methods. Identity theft occurs when someone uses your personal information (i.e.: name, Social Security number, credit card number, etc.) without your permission, to commit fraudulent crimes. No matter what they use your personal information for; the primary crime is considered Identity Theft. Crimes such as obtaining a credit card through illegal methods, using someone else's credit card or establishing accounts and services using someone else's identity are just a few of the identity theft methods used. If I were to list all of the (currently) known methods of identity theft in this book, many of them would be obsolete by the time this book made it to the shelves. That is how quickly identity theft evolves. With technology, thieves are finding new and more high tech ways to steal your information. Whatever methods thieves use to steal your information, can be rendered useless if you proactively protect your information at all times.

Identity thieves prey on people who are careless with their personal, credit card and account information. That's not to say that people who are protective of their personal information are not subject to identity theft. I can confirm that cautious people are sometimes victimized as well. Thieves simply find it easier to prey on those who are not as careful with their personal information.

How do thieves use my personal information once they have access to it?

Thieves can cause many problems once they have access to your personal information, such as:

Credit Card Fraud

- ✓Opening credit card accounts in your name.
- ✓Using your credit card (Possibly maxing it out)
- ✓Selling your credit card to others

Finance Fraud

- ✓Opening a bank account in your name
- ✓Applying for a loan in your name
- ✓Getting access to your ATM card and withdrawing money from your account.
- ✓Transferring money from your accounts
- ✓Selling your information to others

Governmental/Federal Fraud

- ✓Obtaining a drivers license or official ID
- ✓Using your social security number
- ✓Selling your social security number to others
- ✓Accessing your tax return
- ✓Obtaining a job
- ✓Obtaining governmental benefits
- ✓Giving your id to police during an arrest

Other Fraud

- ✓Opening utility accounts in your name (phone, electricity, cable, etc)
- ✓Reporting a cell phone as lost or stolen and get a replacement phone in your name.

A thief can accomplish just about anything that you can think of, with access to your personal information. Remember that we're talking about thieves here. They have a network of people that assist them with their crimes. Let's make it as difficult as possible for thieves to steal your personal information.

What are some of the methods used by Identity Thieves?

Following are just a few of the standard methods used to obtain personal information. These methods are also known as identity theft "scams":

Stealing

One of the oldest methods of identity theft is still one of the most prevalent; stealing. Thieves steal everything from credit cards to mail, statements, purses, wallets and use that information as their own, until they are caught. There is now even the threat of employees stealing information from companies and using it for their benefit.

Phishing
Various methods are used to get you to divulge your personal information such as pop-up messages, spam, pretending to be reputable company or financial institution or etc.

Changing Your Address
Your mail is diverted to an alternate location by simply completing a change of address form. Thieves can then receive and open your mail.

Dumpster Diving
Thieves look for documents that include your personal information in your trash. This can happen at your home or even at a garbage dump site.

Skimming
This is one of the more high tech methods. Thieves use a custom storage device attached to bank machines, which steal your credit and debit card numbers during a regular transaction.

What should I do if my credit or debit card or is lost or stolen?

Following are the steps you should take if you find that your credit card is lost or stolen. It also applies to cases of general identity theft:

1) *Contact the issuer to cancel your credit and debit cards and close any credit accounts affected.*

Most banks have 24 hour services that are dedicated to identity theft and fraud. You should be aware that once you have reported the theft of your credit card, you have no more responsibility for unauthorized charges, according to US law. In addition, your maximum liability under federal law is only $50.00 per credit card.

2) Order new cards and open new accounts
Self explanatory... but do it right away!

3) Report the theft to the lender's Fraud Department
Once you've cancelled your cards and accounts and had them reissued, ask to speak with someone in the issuer's security or fraud department. File an official report directly with them. Make sure the representative sends you the proper fraud dispute forms. You will need these to dispute any charges made by the thief. Once the issue has been resolved, be sure to ask for a letter from the company stating that all of the fraudulent charges have been discharged.

4) Put a fraud alert on your credit
Fraud alerts are offered through the three main credit bureaus. They help prevent thieves from opening new accounts in your name. There are two types of fraud alerts: an initial alert, and an extended alert. An initial fraud alert stays on your credit report for at least 90 days. An extended fraud alert stays on your credit report for seven years. Extended alerts are placed on your credit report if you've been a victim of identity theft and you provide the credit bureau with an Identity Theft Report. Check each credit bureaus individual websites for detailed information regarding fraud alerts and Identity Theft Reports. You only need to contact one of the three credit bureaus to place a fraud alert on your credit. The company you contact is required to contact the other two companies. You should receive a confirmation once the fraud alert is completed as well as one free copy of your credit report.

TransUnion
1-800-680-7289
Fraud Victim Assistance Division
www.transunion.com;
P.O. Box 6790, Fullerton, CA 92834-6790

Equifax
1-800-525-6285
Fraud Division
www.equifax.com;
P.O. Box 740241, Atlanta, GA 30374-0241

Experian
1-888-397-3742
Fraud Division
www.experian.com
P.O. Box 9532, Allen, TX 75013

5) Put a freeze on your credit
Freezing your credit allows you to restrict certain access to your credit report. Thieves would then be unable to gain access to your credit and it will not affect your credit score. You will have to lift the freeze in order for potential lenders and others to gain access to your credit report. Check your particular state for the rules regarding credit freezes. Some states require you to pay a fee and some states offer it as a service to victims of identity theft. Contact the three credit bureaus to request that a freeze be put on your account; however, you should check your state website before doing so. If your state does not allow you to freeze your credit as a free service to identity theft victims, be prepared to pay each of the three agencies if there is a fee required.

6) File an Identity Theft Report with the police
Contact your local police and file a report regarding your identity theft. You will need to file an Identity Theft Report. An Identity Theft Report is a report that you file with the police after your identity has been stolen; however, this report contains more detail than a regular police report. The credit bureaus and companies affected use this detailed report to verify your claims of identity theft, including account numbers and transactions made by the thief versus your transactions.

Checking your credit at least twice per year also helps detect identity theft. You should also review your monthly accounts, bills and statements very closely to ensure that no one is accessing your personal information. I was like many people who found that their identity had been stolen only after the thief had accessed my credit. Fortunately the proactive measures kept them from having complete access to my credit. Put proactive measures in place to protect your credit and personal information. More than anything... be aware!

Following are some tips that should help you protect yourself.

21 Tips to Help Protect You From Theft, Scams and Fraud

1. Buy a cross cutting shredder.
Shredders have come down in cost. Shop around for the best deal for your budget but make sure it is a cross cutting shredder.

2. Shred credit card applications, receipts or anything with your credit card number on it as soon as possible.
"Dumpster divers" can get all of the information they need to steal your identity from one credit card application or bill.

3. Do not carry around credit or debit cards if you do not use them on a daily basis.
Why carry them around if you don't need them. And if you are following your budget, you should not need them on a daily basis.

4. Never give your vital information or credit card information over the phone or via email unless you initiated the call.
The person calling may say they are from a certain company, but how do you know that is true? Get a number and call them back to verify first.

5. Don't let your credit card out of your sight if possible.
When you give your credit card to someone, keep an eye on it while they are using it if possible. In some cases it is not possible; however, be sure to get your card back as quickly as possible when you cannot view it.

6. Never let anyone use your debit or credit card!
If you choose to lend your credit to someone, YOU should make whatever transaction is needed. Do not give your credit card to anyone. Of course, you could avoid all of this by NEVER lending credit.

7. Do not provide your credit card information over a website that is not secure.
All secure websites have an icon that notifies you that you are entering a secure site. Also, keep detailed records when you make purchases online, including confirmation numbers, emails and info.

8. Put passwords on all of your accounts.
Do not use passwords that are easily identifiable (i.e.: your children's names, your pet's name, your maiden name, etc.)

9. Beware of "Shoulder Surfers" at ATMs.
Shoulder surfers peak over your shoulders at ATMS or at stores and get your account, PIN or credit card number instantly. These thieves can capture your information via cell phone or camera, duplicate your cards and use them fraudulently.

10. Never provide your credit or debit card information to anyone who asks for it via email.
"Phishing Scams" are big business, especially in some third world countries. People email asking for credit card information for some "scam" or they ask you to verify your credit card information in order to steal it. Do not respond to these emails. In fact, delete these emails right away!

11. Monitor your account statements carefully each month.
Verify that all purchases were made by you. Also verify your rate and credit limit information.

12. Opt-out of promotional lists and pre-approved offers.
Take your name off all promotional lists by calling the three credit bureaus to "OPT-OUT". You can opt-out via telephone or in writing. Be aware that telephone requests last for two years; however, written requests are permanent. To opt-out via phone, call (888) 5 OPT OUT (888-567-8688). You can be excluded from Experian, Equifax, and TransUnion's promotional lists by accessing that one number.

13. Do not put your telephone number or social security number on checks.
If someone needs this information, they should request it while you are making the transaction.

14. Sign your credit and debit cards as soon as you receive them.
An unsigned card is an open invitation to thieves.

15. Get credit cards with your picture on them.
If you have the option, choose to put your picture on your credit cards. This stops a thief from using your card at many places.

16. NEVER sign a blank credit card receipt.
Doing this gives a thief cart Blanche to your account. Also remember to draw a line through blank sections of receipts where additional tips or charges could be added.

17. Do not use a debit card when shopping online.
Debit cards allow immediate access to your cash. If stolen, thieves can wreak havoc on your account throwing your budget into frenzy before you even know it.

18. Never write your PIN number anywhere near your debit or credit card.
If your wallet gets stolen, thieves have your PIN and all access to your accounts.

19. Place fraud alerts on your cards and credit accounts.
Be proactive about identity theft. Place these alerts on your bank accounts and credit cards to protect yourself in the event that a thief steals your information.

20. Report lost or stolen debit and credit cards IMMEDIATELY!
Give thieves as little time as possible to use your cards.

21. Do not leave receipts at ATMs, gas stations or restaurants.
Thieves can ascertain your personal information from these receipts.

Homework (Session 16)

Identity theft and fraud are no fun. Be proactive in your protection.

Complete the homework for Session 16 in your workbook or e-book.

CONGRATULATIONS!

YOU COMPLETED YOUR CUSTOMIZED PLAN! I am very proud of you and you should be quite proud of yourself.

Before you go....
I want to challenge you to take your financial journey to the next level. Think you're up to the challenge? You purchased this book because you wanted to change your situation, correct? Well... now it's time to put your money where your mouth is. I have a couple of challenges for you... serious challenges. I dare you to take the Wealth Builder's Credit Card and Debit Card challenge. In fact, I double dare you!

Wealth Builder's CREDIT Card Challenge

Here's the challenge!

Unless you pay bills with your credit card, you should not have any monthly credit card requirements. Some people pay certain bills via credit card in order to earn the promotional points from the credit card lender. Other than that, if you have monthly credit card requirements... you need to come and see me for an EMERGENCY in office consultation: something is horribly wrong with your budget.

1) Gather all of your personal (not business) credit cards, find a secure place to hide them at your home and put them away for one month.

2) UNDER NO CIRCUMSTANCE ARE YOU ALLOWED TO USE THAT CREDIT CARD!

3) Document any expenses and potential impulse buys for the challenge month.

4) Keep a small notepad with you to document every impulse or emergency buy that you **almost** purchase for the duration of the two week challenge. *(Most people are in the checkout isle before remembering that they don't have their credit card with them)*

5) At the end of the one month period, review your notes to see how much money you saved and document that. Challenge yourself to save even more during the next challenge!

What will you learn from this challenge?
This challenge will illustrate your judgment in recognizing wants versus needs. Some of our needs quickly become wants when there is no access to ready credit. Credit card spending is out of control and you can only gauge where you are by testing yourself. It's simply too easy to pull that credit card out for unnecessary items. Always ask yourself is this purchase "REQUIRED" or just "DESIRED".

*** *CREDIT CARD TIP* ***

Take your credit building plan to the next level! Integrate this into your annual financial management routine at least four times per year. It's a great way to keep your credit card spending in line while adding to your bottom line.

Wealth Builder's DEBIT Card Challenge

Think you're ready to step up to the plate? Let's see if you make it through the Wealth Builder's Debit Card Challenge.

Here's the challenge!

1) You should already have a monthly budget, broken down into weekly expenses. Write down all of your expenses for two weeks and identify your grand total.

2) Pay the required bills (via check, online or automated) and withdraw any other miscellaneous expenses (i.e.: gas, food, miscellaneous).

3) Here is the key task... put your debit card away for the remainder of the two week challenge *(a full 13 days from the time you start the challenge)*. That means hide it in your home somewhere, not in your car or at your job.

4) UNDER NO CIRCUMSTANCE ARE YOU ALLOWED TO USE THAT DEBIT CARD!

5) Keep a small notepad with you to document every impulse or emergency buy that you **almost** purchase for the duration of the two week challenge. *(Most people are in the checkout isle before remembering that they don't have their debit card with them)*

6) At the end of the two week period, review your notes to see how much money you saved and document that. Challenge yourself to save even more during the next challenge!

What will you learn from this challenge?
This is a great lesson on impulse spending! It will show you just how easy it is to whip out that debit card without tallying up the real damage to your budget/plan. This challenge simply emphasizes the rampant debit card use that has many Americans in debt and in a personal credit crisis!

*** *DEBIT CARD TIP* ***

Use this as a regular wealth building tool by practicing this technique at least two weeks per month.

A Personal Message...

To You

One of the things that prompted me to write this book was the lack of comprehensive information regarding the credit process. I saw a lot of books on the bookshelves about one portion of the credit process and a little about another portion, but none of them offered enough information about the true inner workings of the full process. I did a great deal of research for this book and found that many of the books regarding credit had titles that preyed on the general public's fears and anxieties regarding credit. In fact, as I write this book, in early 2009, it seems that America, in its entirety, is gripped with fear regarding the state of credit and the economy in the U.S. Unfortunately, there are opportunistic people who take advantage of that fear by harping on it to sell product. Well... I am here to tell you that there is ABSOLUTELY no reason to fear the credit process or this economic downturn.

Please understand that fear is one of the most powerful and dangerous emotions one can have. Fear can cause you to be non-productive and apathetic about your situation, thereby rendering you paralyzed and helpless... IF YOU ALLOW IT! You have a choice about your future, no matter what state your credit or finances are in. You must simply manage and control what is in your power and let anything that is out of your control roll off your back like water on a duck. Why worry about it, if it's out of your control? Will worrying turn the economy around? Will fear about your credit history change that history? The answer, of course, is absolutely not.

My sincere desire is to educate you about the ins and outs of the credit process. It is vitally important for you to have the history, data and information that will help put you on an even playing field. Why do most people have fear: lack of knowledge and anxiety about the unknown? I pray that the information in this book helped to eradicate your lack of credit knowledge and as I said, you should never be fearful of what "may or may not" happen. If you're living in fear for tomorrow, you'll never enjoy your life today. Our motto moving forward is: NO FEAR THIS YEAR! Say it with me... NO FEAR THIS YEAR!

Peace and Blessings to you while you continue your journey of personal and financial happiness.

Sincerely,

Your Friend,
Brian P. Willis, President
Wealth Builders Enterprises, Inc.

Bibliography

2003 Changes to the Fair Credit Reporting Act: Important Steps Forward at a High Cost, ConsumersUnion.org http://www.consumersunion.org/pub/core_financial_services/000745.html

Edelman, Ric. The Truth About Money. Washington, DC: Georgetown University, 1996.

Equifax Company History, http://equifax.com. 2 Jan. 2009

Experian Company History, http://www.experian.com. 12 Jan. 2009

Federal Trade Commission, www.ftc.gov/credits and loans. 23 Jan. 2009

FICO, http://www.myfico.com/CreditEducation/InYourReport.aspx. 7 Jan. 2009

Fumiko, Hyashi, Sullivan Richard, Weiner, Stuart E. The History of ATM and Debit. Kansas City, Mo, 2003

TransUnion Company History, http://transunion.com. 10 Jan. 2009

Rothbard, Murray N. America's Great Depression Fifth Edition. Auburn, AL: Ludwig von Mises Institute, 2000

Coburn, Karen and Madge Treeger. Letting Go: A Parents' Guide to Understanding the College Years. New York: HarperCollins Publishers, 2003.

Soros, George. The New Paradigm for Financial Markets. Philadelphia, PA; Perseus Books Group, 2008

Small Business Dictionary, Business Dictionary, http://www.businessdictionary.com/definition/credit.html. 23 Jan. 2009

Stanley, Thomas J., and William D. Danko. The Millionaire Next Door. New York: Pocket Books, 1998.

U.S. Census Bureau; Finance and Insurance, 2002 (POD Report), 2008.

Vantage Score, http://www.vantagescore.com/about. 5 Jan. 2009

Webster Online, http://www.merriam-webster.com/dictionary. 20 Jan. 2009

Acknowledgements

There are always numerous people and organizations that contribute to anyone's success. I would like to acknowledge some of the people and organizations that have been an inspiration to me:

- *James J. Dozier (JJ)*
- *Ms. Ruth and Another Choice Adoption Agency*
- *100 Black Men of Charlotte*
- *Dr. Sheldon R. Shipman and Greenville Memorial A.M.E. Zion Church*
- *The Urban League of Charlotte*
- *Maurice Wilson and Wilson Wealth Management*
- *Thifty Kids Organization (TKO)*
- *All of my friends and family*